INTIMACY

INTIMACY

Trusting Oneself
and the Other

osho

·

insights for a
new way of living

St. Martin's Griffin ⋈ New York

www.stmartins.com

Editing and compilation by Wendy Champagne

Library of Congress Cataloging-in-Publication Data

Osho, 1931–1990.
    Intimacy : trusting oneself and the other / Osho.
        p. cm.
    ISBN-13: 978-0-312-27566-2
    ISBN-10: 0-312-27566-8
    1. Intimacy (Psychology)—Religious aspects. I. Title.

BP605.R34 O738 2001
299'.93—dc21

                                                    2001049012

First St. Martin's Griffin Edition: December 2001

10 9 8

Contents

Contents

Foreword

Everybody is afraid of intimacy—it is another thing whether you are aware of it or not. Intimacy means exposing yourself before a stranger—and we are all strangers; nobody knows anybody. We are even strangers to ourselves because we don't know who we are.

Intimacy brings you close to a stranger. You have to drop all your defenses; only then is intimacy possible. And the fear is that if you drop all your defenses, all your masks, who knows what the stranger will do with you? We are all hiding a thousand and one things, not only from others but from ourselves, because we have been brought up by a sick humanity with all kinds of repressions, inhibitions, taboos. And the fear is that with somebody who is a stranger—and it does not matter, you may have lived with the person for thirty years, forty years; the strangeness never disappears—it feels safer to keep a little defense, a little distance, because somebody can take advantage of your weaknesses, of your frailties, of your vulnerability.

> You have to drop all your defenses; only then is intimacy possible. We are all hiding a thousand and one things, not only from others but from ourselves.

Everybody is afraid of intimacy.

The problem becomes more complicated because everybody wants intimacy. Everybody wants intimacy because otherwise you are alone in this universe—without a friend, without a lover, without anybody you can trust, without anybody to whom you can open all your wounds. And the wounds cannot heal unless they are open. The more you hide them, the more dangerous they become. They can become cancerous.

Intimacy is an essential need on the one hand, so everybody longs for it. You want the other person to be intimate so that the other person drops his defenses, becomes vulnerable, opens all his wounds, drops all his masks and false personality, stands naked as he is. And on the other hand, everybody is afraid of intimacy—you want to be intimate with the other person, but you are not dropping your defenses. This is one of the conflicts between friends, between lovers: Nobody wants to drop his defenses, and nobody wants to come in utter nudity and sincerity, open—yet both need intimacy.

Unless you drop all your repressions and inhibitions—which are the gifts of your religions, your cultures, your societies, your parents, your education—you will never be able to be intimate with someone. And you will have to take the initiative.

But if you don't have any repressions or inhibitions, then you don't have any wounds, either. If you have lived a simple, natural life, there will be no fear of intimacy, only the tremendous joy of two flames coming so close that they become almost one flame. And the meeting is tremendously gratifying, satisfying, fulfilling. But before you can attempt intimacy, you have to clean your house completely.

Only a man of meditation can allow intimacy to happen. He has nothing to hide. All that was making him afraid that somebody may know, he himself has dropped. He has only a silence and a loving heart.

You have to accept yourself in your totality. If you cannot accept yourself in your totality, how can you expect somebody else to accept you? And you have been condemned by everybody, and you have learned only one thing: self-condemnation. You go on hiding it; it is not something beautiful to show to others. You know ugly things are hidden in you, you know evil things are hidden in you, you know animality is hidden in you. Unless you transform your attitude and accept yourself as one of the animals in existence . . .

The word *animal* is not bad. It simply means alive; it comes from *anima*. Whoever is alive is an animal. But man has been taught, "You are not animals; animals are far below you. You are human beings." You have been given a false superiority. The truth is, existence does not believe in the superior and the inferior. To existence, everything is equal: the trees, the birds, the animals, the human beings. In existence, everything is absolutely accepted as it is; there is no condemnation.

If you accept your sexuality without any conditions, if you accept that man and every being in the world is fragile, that life is a very thin thread that can break down any moment . . . Once this is accepted, and you drop false egos—of being Alexander the Great, Muhammad Ali the thrice-great— you simply understand that everybody is beautiful in his ordinariness and everyone has weaknesses; they are part of human nature because you are not made of steel. You are made of a very fragile body. The span of your life is between ninety-eight degrees and one hundred ten degrees, just twelve degrees of temperature is your whole span of life. Fall below it and you are dead; go beyond it and you are dead. And

> If you are ready to be intimate, you will encourage the other person also to be intimate. Your unpretentious simplicity will allow the other also to enjoy simplicity, innocence, trust, love, openness.

the same applies to a thousand and one things in you. One of your most basic needs is to be needed. But nobody wants to accept that "it is my basic need to be needed, to be loved, to be accepted."

We are living in such pretensions, such hypocrisies—that is why intimacy creates fear. You are not what you appear to be. Your appearance is false. You may appear to be a saint, but deep down you are still a weak human being with all the desires and all the longings.

> The truth is, existence does not believe in the superior and the inferior. In existence, everything is absolutely accepted as it is; there is no condemnation.

The first step is to accept yourself in your totality—in spite of all your traditions, which have driven the whole of humanity insane. Once you have accepted yourself as you are, the fear of intimacy will disappear. You cannot lose respect, you cannot lose your greatness, you cannot lose your ego. You cannot lose your piousness, you cannot lose your saintliness—you have dropped all that yourself. You are just like a small child, utterly innocent. You can open yourself because inside you are not filled with ugly repressions that have become perversions. You can say everything that you feel authentically and sincerely. And if you are ready to be intimate, you will encourage the other person also to be intimate. Your openness will help the other person also to be open to you. Your unpretentious simplicity will allow the other also to enjoy simplicity, innocence, trust, love, openness.

You are encaged with stupid concepts, and the fear is that if you become very intimate with somebody, he will become aware of it. But we are fragile beings—the most fragile in the whole existence. The human child is the most fragile child of all the animals. The children of other animals can survive without the mother, without the father, without a family. But the human child will die immediately. So this frailty is not something to be condemned—it is the highest expression of consciousness. A rose flower is going to be fragile; it is not a stone. And there is no need to feel bad that you are a rose flower and not a stone.

Only when two persons become intimate are they no longer strangers. And it is a beautiful experience to find that not only you are full of weaknesses but the other, too—perhaps everybody—is full of weaknesses. The higher expression of anything becomes weaker. The roots are very strong, but the flower cannot be so strong. Its beauty is because of its not being strong. In the morning it opens its petals to welcome the sun, dances the whole day in the wind, in the rain, in the sun, and by the evening its petals have started falling; it is gone.

Everything that is beautiful, precious, is going to be very momentary. But you want everything to be permanent. You love someone and you promise, "I will love you my whole life." And you know perfectly well that you cannot be even certain of tomorrow—you are giving a false promise. All that you can say is, "I am in love with you this moment, and I will give my totality to you. About the next moment, I know nothing. How can I promise? You have to forgive me."

But lovers are promising all kinds of things they cannot fulfill. Then frustration comes in; then the distance grows bigger; then fight, conflict, struggle, and a life that was meant to become happier becomes just a long, drawn-out misery.

If you become aware that you are afraid of intimacy, it can become a great revelation to you, and a revolution if you look inward and start dropping everything of which you feel ashamed and accept your nature as it is, not as it should be. I do not teach any "should." All shoulds make the human mind sick. People should be taught the beauty of *isness,* the tremendous splendor of nature. The trees don't know any Ten Commandments, the birds don't know any Holy Scriptures. It is only man who has created a problem for himself. Condemning your own nature, you become split, you become schizophrenic.

And not just ordinary people but people of the status of Sigmund Freud, who contributed greatly to humanity's understanding of the mind. His method was psychoanalysis, that you should be made aware of all that is unconscious in you. And this is the secret: Once something unconscious is brought to the conscious mind, it evaporates. You become cleaner, lighter. As more and more of the unconscious is unburdened, your consciousness goes on becoming bigger. And as the area of the unconscious shrinks, the territory of the consciousness expands.

That is an immense truth. The East has known it for thousands of years, but in the West, Sigmund Freud introduced it—not knowing anything of the East and its psychology. It was his individual contribution. But you will be surprised to know that he was never ready to be psychoanalyzed himself. The founder of psychoanalysis was never psychoanalyzed. His colleagues insisted again and again, "You have given us the method, and we all have been psychoanalyzed. Why are you insisting that you should not be psychoanalyzed?"

He said, "Forget about it." He was afraid to expose himself. He had become a great genius, and exposing himself would bring him down to ordinary humanity. He had the same fears, the same desires, the same repressions. He never talked about his dreams, he only listened to other people's dreams. And his colleagues were very much surprised—"It will be a great contribution to know about your dreams." But he never agreed to lie down on the psychoanalyst's couch and talk about his dreams because his dreams were as ordinary as anybody else's—that was the fear.

A Gautam Buddha would not have feared to go into meditation—that was his contribution, a special kind of meditation. And he would not have been afraid of any psychoanalysis because for the man who meditates, by and by all his dreams disappear. In the day he remains silent in his mind, not the ordinary traffic of thoughts. And in the night he sleeps deeply because dreams are nothing but unlived thoughts, unlived desires, unlived longings from the day. They are trying to complete themselves, at least in dreams.

It will be very difficult for you to find a man who dreams about his wife or a woman who dreams about her husband. But it will be absolutely common that they dream about their neighbors' wives and their neighbors' husbands. The wife is available; the husband is not suppressing anything as far as his wife is concerned. But the neighbor's wife is always more beautiful, the grass is always greener on the other side of the fence. And that which is unapproachable creates a deep desire to acquire it, to possess it. In the day you cannot do it, but in dreams at least you are free. Freedom to dream has not yet been taken away by governments.

It won't be long—soon they will take it away because methods are available, already available, so that they can watch when you are dreaming and when you are not dreaming. And there is a possibility someday to find a scientific device so that your dream can be projected on a screen. Some electrodes will just have to be inserted in your head. You will be fast asleep, dreaming joyously, making love to your neighbor's wife, and a whole movie hall will be watching it. And they used to think this man was a saint!

This much you can even see: Whenever a person is asleep, watch; if his eyelids are not showing any movement of his eyes inside, then he is not dreaming. If he is dreaming, then you can see that his eyes are moving.

It may one day be possible to project your dream on a screen. It may also be possible to enforce certain dreaming in you. But at least up until now, no constitution even talks about it, that "People are free to dream; it is their birthright."

A Gautam Buddha does not dream. Meditation is a way to go beyond mind. He lives in utter silence twenty-four hours—no ripples on the lake of his consciousness, no thoughts, no dreams.

But a Sigmund Freud is afraid because he knows what he is dreaming.

I have heard about an incident. Three great Russian novelists—Chekhov, Gorky, and Tolstoy—were just sitting on a bench in a park and gossiping; they were great friends. All were geniuses, all created such great novels that even today, if you want to count ten great novels of the world, at least five will be from the Russian novelists before the revolution.

Chekhov was telling about the women in his life, Gorky joined in, he also said a few things. But Tolstoy remained silent. Tolstoy was a very orthodox, religious Christian. You will be surprised to know that Mahatma Gandhi in India has accepted three persons as his masters, and one was Tolstoy.

And he must have been repressing so much. He was one of the richest men in Russia—he was a member of the nobility—but he lived like a poor beggar because "blessed are the poor and they shall inherit the kingdom of God," and he was not willing to give up the kingdom of God. This is not simplicity, and it is not desirelessness—it is too much desire. It is too much greed. It is too much instinct for power. He is sacrificing this life and its joys because it is a small life, and for eternity he will enjoy paradise and the kingdom of God. It is a good bargain—almost like a lottery but certain.

Tolstoy was living a very celibate life, eating only vegetarian food.

He was almost a saint! Naturally his dreams must have been very ugly, his thoughts must have been very ugly. And when Chekhov and Gorky asked him, "Tolstoy, why are you silent? Say something!" He said, "I cannot say anything about women. I will say something only when one foot is in the grave. I will say it, and then jump into the grave."

You can understand why he was so afraid of saying anything; it was boiling within him. Now, you cannot be very intimate with a man like Tolstoy. . . .

Intimacy simply means that the doors of the heart are open for you; you are welcome to come in and be a guest. But that is possible only if you have a heart that is not stinking with repressed sexuality, that is not boiling with all kinds of perversions, a heart that is natural. As natural as trees, as innocent as children—then there is no fear of intimacy.

That's what I am trying to do: to help you unburden your unconscious, unburden your mind, to become ordinary. There is nothing more beautiful than to be just simple and ordinary. Then you can have as many intimate friends, as many intimate relationships, as possible because you are not afraid of anything. You become an open book that anybody can read. There is nothing to hide.

Every year, a hunting club went up into the Montana hills. The members drew straws to decide who would handle the cooking and also agreed that anyone complaining about the food would automatically replace the unlucky cook.

Realizing after a few days that no one was likely to risk speaking up, Sanderson decided on a desperate plan. He found some moose droppings and added two handfuls to the stew that night. There were grimaces around the campfire after the first few mouthfuls, but nobody said anything. Then one member suddenly broke the silence. "Hey," he exclaimed, "this stuff tastes like moose shit—but good!"

You have so many faces. Inside, you think one thing; outside, you express something else. You are not one organic whole.

Relax and destroy the split that society has created in you. Say only that which you mean. Act according to your own spontaneity, never bothering about consequences. It is a small life, and it should not be spoiled in thinking about consequences here and hereafter.

One should live totally, intensely, joyously and just like an open book, available for anybody to read it. Of course you will not make a name in the history books. But what is the point in making a name in the history books?

> Say only that which you mean. It is a small life, and it should not be spoiled in thinking about consequences here and hereafter.

Live, rather than think of being remembered. You will be dead.

Millions of people have lived on the earth, and we don't know even their names. Accept that simple fact—you are here for only a few days and then you will be gone. These few days are not to be wasted in hypocrisy, in fear. These days have to be rejoiced.

Nobody knows anything about the future. Your heaven and your hell and your God are most probably all hypotheses, unproved. The only thing that is in your hands is your life—make it as rich as possible.

By intimacy, by love, by opening yourself to many people, you become richer. And if you can live in deep love, in deep friendship, in deep intimacy, with many people, you have lived rightly. And

> Millions of people have lived on the earth, and we don't know even their names. Accept that simple fact—you are here for only a few days and then you will be gone. These few days are not to be wasted in hypocrisy, in fear.

wherever you happen to be, you have learned the art, and you will be living happily there, too.

If you are simple, loving, open, intimate, you create a paradise around you. If you are closed, constantly on the defensive, always worried that somebody may come to know your thoughts, your dreams, your perversions, you are living in hell. Hell is within you—and so is paradise. They are not geographical places, they are your spiritual spaces.

Cleanse yourself. And meditation is nothing but a cleaning of all the rubbish that has gathered in your mind. When the mind is silent and the heart is singing, you will be ready—without any fear but with great joy—to be intimate. And without intimacy, you are alone here among strangers. With intimacy, you are surrounded by friends, by people who love you. Intimacy is a great experience. One should not miss it.

FIRST THINGS FIRST
THE ABC OF INTIMACY

People are searching for meditation, prayer, new ways of being. But the deeper search, and the more basic search, is how to get rooted in existence again. Call it meditation, call it prayer, or whatever you will, but the essential thing is how to get rooted in existence again. We have become trees that are uprooted—and nobody else is responsible except us, with our own stupid idea of conquering nature.

We are part of nature—how can the part conquer the whole? Befriend it, love it, trust it, and slowly, slowly in that friendship, in that love, in that trust, intimacy arises; you come closer. Nature comes closer to you, and nature starts revealing its secrets. Its ultimate secret is godliness. It is revealed only to those who are really friends of existence.

START WHERE YOU ARE

Life is a search—a constant search, a desperate search, a hopeless search, a search for something one knows not what. There is a deep urge to seek, but one knows not what one is seeking. And there is a certain state of mind in which whatsoever you get is not going to give you any satisfaction. Frustration seems to be the destiny of humanity because whatsoever you get becomes meaningless the very moment you have it. You start searching again.

The search continues whether you get anything or not. It seems irrelevant—what you have, what you don't have, the search continues anyway. The poor are searching, the rich are searching, the ill are searching, the well are searching, the powerful are searching, the powerless are searching, the stupid are searching, the wise are searching—and nobody knows exactly what for.

This very search—what it is and why it is there—has to be understood. It seems that there is a gap in the human being, in the human mind. In the very structure of the human consciousness there seems to be a hole, a black hole. You go on throwing things into it, and they go on disappearing. Nothing seems to make it full, nothing seems to help toward fulfillment. It is a very feverish search. You seek it in this world, you seek it in the other world. Sometimes you seek it in money, in power, in prestige, and sometimes you seek it in God, bliss, love, meditation, prayer—but the search continues. It seems that man is ill with search.

The search does not allow you to be here and now because the search always leads you somewhere else. The search is a projection, the search is a desire, an idea that somewhere else is what is needed—that it exists, but it exists somewhere else, not here where you are. It certainly exists but not in this moment of time—not now, but somewhere else. It exists then, there, never here now. It goes on nagging you, it goes on pulling you, pushing you. It goes on throwing you into more and more madness; it drives you crazy. And it is never fulfilled.

I have heard about a very great Sufi mystic woman, Rabia al-Adawia:

One evening, as the sun was setting, and there was a little light still left on the road, people found her sitting on the road searching for something. She was an old woman, her eyes were weak, and it was difficult for her to see. So the neighbors came to help her. They asked, "What are you searching for?"

Rabia said, "That question is irrelevant. I am searching— if you can help me, help."

They laughed and said, "Rabia, have you gone mad? You say our question is irrelevant, but if we don't know what you are searching for, how can we help?"

Rabia said, "Okay—just to satisfy you—I am searching for my needle. I have lost my needle." They started helping her but immediately became aware of the fact that the road was very big, and a needle was a very tiny thing.

So they asked Rabia, "Please tell us where you lost it— the exact, precise place—otherwise it is difficult. The road is big, and we can go on searching and searching forever. Where did you lose it?"

Rabia said, "Again you ask an irrelevant question. How is it concerned with my search?"

They stopped and said, "You have certainly gone crazy!"

Rabia said, "Okay—just to satisfy you—I have lost it in my house."

They asked, "Then why are you searching here?"

And Rabia is reported to have said, "Because here there is light, and there is no light inside."

This parable is very significant. Have you ever asked yourself what you are searching for? Have you ever made it a point of deep meditation to know what you are searching for? No. Even if in some vague moments, dreaming moments, you have some inkling of what you are

> ⌇
>
> Have you ever asked yourself what you are searching for? Have you ever made it a point of deep meditation to know what you are searching for?

searching for, it is never precise, it is never exact. You have not yet defined it.

If you try to define it, the more it becomes defined, the more you will feel that there is no need to search for it. The search can continue only in a state of vagueness, in a state of dreaming; when things are not clear, you simply go on searching, pulled by some inner urge, pushed by some inner urgency. One thing you do know: You need to search. This is an inner need. But you don't know what you are seeking. And unless you know what you are seeking, how can you find it?

It is vague—you think the key is in money, power, prestige, respectability. But then you see people who are respectable, people who are powerful, and they are also seeking. Then you see people who are tremendously rich, and they are also seeking; to the very end of their lives they are seeking. So richness is not going to help, power is not going to help. The search continues in spite of what you have.

The search must be for something else. These names, these labels—money, power, prestige—these are just to satisfy your mind. They are just to help you feel that you are searching for something. That something is still undefined, a very vague feeling.

The first thing for the real seeker—for the seeker who has become a little alert, aware—is to define the search, to formulate a clear-cut concept of what it is, to bring it out of the dreaming consciousness, to encounter it in deep alertness, to look into it directly; to face it. Immediately a transformation starts happening. If you start defining

4

your search, you will start losing your interest in the search. The more defined it becomes, the less it is there. Once it is clearly known what it is, suddenly it disappears. It exists only when you are not attentive.

Let it be repeated: The search exists only when you are sleepy. The search exists only when you are not aware; the search exists only in your unawareness. The unawareness creates the search.

Yes, Rabia is right. Inside there is no light—and since there is no light and no consciousness inside, of course you go on searching outside because outside it seems more clear.

Our senses are all extroverted. The eyes open outward, the hands move, spread outward, the legs move into the outside, the ears listen to the outside noises, to sounds. Whatsoever is available to you is all opening to the outside; all the five senses move in an extroverted way. You start searching there—where you see, feel, touch. The light of the senses falls outside, and the seeker is inside.

This dichotomy has to be understood. The seeker is inside—but because the light is outside, the seeker starts moving in an ambitious way, trying to find something outside that will be fulfilling. It is never going to happen. It has never happened. It cannot happen in the nature of things because unless you have sought the seeker, all your search is meaningless. Unless you come to know who you are, all that you seek is futile because you don't know the seeker. Without knowing the seeker, how can you move in the right dimension, in the right direction? It is impossible. The first things should be considered first.

So these two things are very important: First, make it absolutely clear to yourself what your object is. Don't just go on stumbling in darkness. Focus your attention on the object: What are you really searching for? Because sometimes you want one thing, and you go on searching for something else, so even if you succeed you will not be fulfilled. Have you seen people who have succeeded? Can you find bigger failures anywhere else? You have heard the proverb that nothing succeeds like success. It is absolutely wrong. I would like to tell you, nothing fails like success. The proverb must have been invented by stupid people. I repeat: Nothing fails like success.

It is said about Alexander the Great that the day he became the world conqueror, he closed the doors of his room and started weeping. I don't know whether it really happened or not, but if he was even a little intelligent, it must have happened. His generals were very disturbed:

What had happened? They had never seen Alexander weeping. He was not that type of man; he was a great warrior. They had seen him in great difficulties, in situations where life was very much in danger, where death was very imminent, and they had not seen even a tear coming out of his eyes. They had never seen him in any desperate, hopeless moment. What has happened to him now . . . when he has succeeded, when he is the world conqueror?

They knocked on the door, they went in, and they asked, "What has happened to you? Why are you crying like a child?"

He said, "Now that I have succeeded, I know it has been a failure. Now I know that I stand exactly in the same place as I used to be when I started this nonsense of conquering the world. And the point has become clear to me now because there is no other world to conquer; otherwise, I could have remained on the journey, I could have started conquering another world. Now there is no other world to conquer, now there is nothing else to do—and suddenly I am thrown to myself."

A successful man is always thrown to himself in the end, and then he suffers the tortures of hell because he wasted his whole life. He searched and searched, he staked everything that he had. Now he is successful, and his heart is empty, and his soul is meaningless, and there is no fragrance, there is no benediction.

So the first thing is to know exactly what you are seeking. I insist upon it—because the more you focus your eyes on the object of your search, the more the object starts disappearing. When your eyes are absolutely fixed, suddenly there is nothing to seek; immediately your eyes start turning toward yourself. When there is no object for search, when all objects have disappeared, there is emptiness. In that emptiness is conversion, turning in. You suddenly start looking at yourself. Now there is nothing to seek, and a new desire arises to know this seeker.

If there is something to seek, you are a worldly man. If there is nothing to seek, and the question "Who is this seeker?" has become important to you, then you are a religious man. This is the way I define the worldly and the religious. If you are still seeking something—maybe in the other life, on the other shore, in heaven, in paradise, it makes no difference—you are still a worldly man. If all seeking has stopped and you have suddenly become aware that now there is only one thing to know—"Who is this seeker in me? What is this energy that wants to seek? Who am I?"—then there is a transformation. All values change suddenly. You start moving

> If all seeking has stopped and you have suddenly become aware that now there is only one thing to know—"Who is this seeker in me? What is this energy that wants to seek? Who am I?"—then there is a transformation.

7

inward. Then Rabia is no longer sitting on the road searching for a needle that is lost somewhere in the darkness of her own inner soul.

Once you have started moving inward . . . In the beginning it is very dark—Rabia is right, it is very, very dark. Because for lives together you have never been inside, your eyes have been focused on the outside world. Have you watched it? Observed? Sometimes when you come in from the road, where it is very sunny and the sun is hot and there is bright light, when you suddenly come into the room or into the house it is very dark—because the eyes are focused for much outside light. When there is much light, the pupils shrink. In darkness the pupils have to relax; a bigger aperture is needed in darkness. In light, a smaller aperture is enough. That's how the camera functions, and that's how your eye functions; the camera has been invented along the lines of the human eye.

So when you suddenly come in from the outside, your own house looks dark. But if you sit a little while, by and by the darkness disappears. There is more light; your eyes are settling. For many lives together you have been outside in the hot sun, in the world, so when you go in you have completely forgotten how to enter and how to readjust your eyes. Meditation is nothing but a readjustment of your vision, a readjustment of your seeing faculty, of your eyes.

In India that is what is called your third eye. It is not an actual eye somewhere, it is a readjustment, a total readjustment of your vision. By and by the darkness is no longer dark. A subtle, suffused light starts being felt. And if you go on looking inside—it takes time—gradually, slowly, you start feeling a beautiful light inside. It is not aggressive light like the sun; it is more like the moon. It is not glaring, it is not dazzling, it is very cool. It is not hot, it is very compassionate, it is very soothing, it is a balm.

By and by, when you have adjusted to the inside light, you will see that you are the very source. The seeker is the sought. Then you will see that the treasure is within you, and the whole problem was that you were seeking for it outside. You were seeking it somewhere outside, and it has always been there inside you. It has always been here within you. You were seeking in a wrong direction, that's all.

Everything is available to you as much as it is available to anyone else, as much as it is available to a Buddha, to a Baal-Shem, to a Moses, to a Muhammad. It is all available to you, only you are looking in the wrong direction. As far as the treasure is concerned, you are not poorer than Buddha or Muhammad—no, God has never created a poor man. It does not happen—it cannot happen because God creates you out of his richness. How can God create a poor man? You are his overflowing; you are part of existence. How can you be poor? You are rich, infinitely rich—as rich as nature itself.

But you are looking in the wrong direction. The direction is wrong. That's why you go on missing. And it is not that you will not succeed in life—you can succeed. But still you will be a failure. Nothing is going to satisfy you because nothing can be attained in the outside world that can be comparable to the inner treasure, to the inner light, to the inner bliss.

SELF-KNOWLEDGE IS POSSIBLE ONLY IN DEEP ALONENESS. Ordinarily whatever we know about ourselves is the opinion of others. They say, "You are good," and we think we are good. They say, "You are beautiful," and we think we are beautiful. They say, "You are bad" or "You are ugly" . . . whatsoever people say about us, we go on collecting. That becomes our self-identity. It is utterly false because nobody else can know you—nobody can know who you are except you, yourself. They know only aspects, and those aspects are very superficial. They know only momentary moods; they cannot penetrate your center. Not even your lover can penetrate to the very core of your being. There you are utterly alone, and only there will you come to know who you are.

People live their whole lives believing in what others say, dependent on others. That's why people are very afraid of others' opinions. If they think you are bad, you become bad. If they condemn you, you start condemning yourself. If they say that you are a sinner, you start feeling guilty. Because you have to depend on their opinions, you have to continuously conform to their ideas; otherwise they will change their opinions. This creates a slavery, a very subtle slavery. If you want to be known as good, worthy, beautiful, intelligent, then you have to concede, you have to compromise continuously with people on whom you are dependent.

> People live their whole lives believing in what others say, dependent on others. That's why people are very afraid of others' opinions. If they think you are bad, you become bad. If they condemn you, you start condemning yourself.

And another problem arises. Because there are so many people, they go on feeding your mind with different types of opinions—conflicting opinions, too. One opinion contradicting another opinion; hence a great confusion exists inside you. One person says you are very intelligent, another person says you are stupid. How to decide? So you are divided. You become suspicious about yourself, about who you are . . . a wavering. And the complexity is very great because there are thousands of people around you.

You come in contact with so many people, and everybody is feeding his idea into your mind. And nobody knows you—not even you yourself know—so all this collection becomes jumbled up inside. This is a maddening situation. You have many voices inside you. Whenever you ask who you are, many answers will come. Some answers will be your mother's, some will be your father's, some will be your teacher's, and so on and so forth. And it is impossible to decide which one is the right answer. How to decide? What is the criterion? This is where man is lost. This is self-ignorance.

But because you depend on others, you are afraid to go into aloneness—because the moment you start going into aloneness, you start becoming very afraid of losing yourself. You don't have yourself in the first place, but whatever self you have created out of others' opinions will have to be left behind. Hence, it is very scary to go in. The deeper you go, the less you know who you are. So in fact when you are moving toward self-knowledge, before it happens you will have to drop all ideas about the self. There will be a gap; there will be a kind of nothingness. You will become a nonentity. You will be utterly lost because all that you know is no longer relevant, and that which is relevant you don't know yet.

Christian mystics call this "the dark night of the soul." It has to be passed, and once you have passed it, there is the dawn. The sun rises, and one comes to know oneself for the first time. The first ray of the sun, and all is fulfilled. The first songs of the birds in the morning, and all is attained.

BE AUTHENTIC

Truthfulness means authenticity—to be true, not to be false, not to use masks. Whatsoever is your real face, show it at whatever the cost.

Remember, that doesn't mean that you have to unmask others; if they are happy with their lies, it is for them to decide. Don't go and unmask anybody because this is how people think—they say they have to be truthful, authentic; they mean they have to go and make everybody nude because "Why are you hiding your body? These clothes are not needed." No. Please remember: Be truthful to yourself. You are not needed to reform anybody else in the world. If you can grow yourself, that's enough. Don't be a reformer, and don't try to teach others, and don't try to change others. If *you* change, that's enough of a message.

> Don't be a reformer, and don't try to teach others, and don't try to change others. If *you* change, that's enough of a message.

To be authentic means to remain true to your own being. How to remain true? Three things have to be remembered. One, never listen to anybody, what they tell you to be. Always listen to your inner voice, what you would like to be; otherwise your whole life will be wasted. Your mother wants you to be an engineer, your father wants you to be a doctor, and you want to be a poet. What to do? Of course the mother is right because it is more economical, more financially helpful, to be an engineer. The father is also right; to be a doctor is a good commodity in the market, it has a market value. A poet? Have you gone mad? Are you crazy? Poets are people who are cursed. Nobody wants them. There is no need for them; the world can exist without poetry—there will be no trouble just because there is no poetry. The world cannot exist without engineers; the world needs engineers. If you are needed, you are valuable. If you are not needed, you don't carry any value.

But if you want to be a poet, be a poet. You may be a beggar—good. You may not become very rich out of it, but don't worry about it. Because otherwise you may become a great engineer, and you may earn much money, but you will never have any fulfillment. You will always hanker; your inner being will hanker to be a poet.

I have heard that one great scientist, a surgeon who was awarded a Nobel Prize, was asked, "When the Nobel Prize was awarded to you, you didn't look very happy. What is the matter?" He said, "I always wanted to be a dancer. I never wanted to be a surgeon in the first place, and now not only have I become a surgeon, I have become a very successful surgeon, and this is a burden. I wanted to be just a dancer, and I remain a lousy dancer—that is my pain, my anguish. Whenever I see somebody dancing, I feel so miserable, in such hell. What will I do with this Nobel Prize? It can't become a dance to me; it can't give me a dance."

Remember, be true to your inner voice. It may lead you into danger; then go in danger, but remain true to the inner voice. Then there is a possibility that one day you will come to a state where you can dance with inner fulfillment.

Always look: The first thing is your being. Don't allow others to manipulate and control you—and they are many; everybody is ready to control you, everybody is ready to change you, everybody is ready to give you a direction you have not asked for. Everybody

> To be authentic means to be true to oneself. It is a very, very dangerous phenomenon, rare people can do that. But whenever people do it, they achieve such beauty, such grace, such contentment that you cannot imagine.

is giving you a guide for your life. The guide exists within you, you carry the blueprint.

To be authentic means to be true to oneself. It is a very, very dangerous phenomenon; rare people can do that. But whenever people do it, they achieve. They achieve such beauty, such grace, such contentment that you cannot imagine.

The reason everybody looks so frustrated is that nobody has listened to his own voice. You wanted to marry a girl, but the girl was a Mohammedan, and you are a Hindu Brahmin, your parents wouldn't allow it. The society wouldn't accept it, it was dangerous. The girl was poor and you are rich. So you married a rich woman, Hindu, Brahmin by caste, accepted by everybody but not by your heart. So now you live an ugly life. Now you go to prostitutes—but even prostitutes won't help you; you have prostituted your whole life. You wasted your whole life.

Always listen to the inner voice, and don't listen to anything else.

> Everybody is a salesman. If you listen to too many salesmen, you will become mad. Don't listen to anybody. Just close your eyes and listen to the inner voice.

There are a thousand and one temptations around you because many people are peddling their things. It is a supermarket, the world, and everybody in it is interested in selling his thing to you. Everybody is a salesman. If you listen to too many salesmen, you will become mad. Don't listen to anybody. Just close your eyes and listen to the inner voice. That is what meditation is all about, to listen to the inner voice. This is the first thing.

Then the second thing—only if you have done the first thing does the second become possible—never wear a mask. If you are angry, be angry. It is risky, but don't smile because that is being untrue. You have been taught that when you are angry, smile, but then your smile becomes false, a mask—just an exercise of the lips and nothing else. The heart full of anger, poison, and the lips smiling; you become a false phenomenon.

Then the other thing also happens: When you want to smile, you cannot smile. Your whole mechanism is topsy-turvy because when you wanted to be angry you weren't; when you wanted to hate you didn't. Now you want to love; suddenly you find that the mechanism doesn't function. Now you want to smile; you have to force it. Really, your heart is full of smile, and you want to laugh out loud, but you cannot laugh. Something chokes in the heart, something chokes in the throat. The smile doesn't come, or even if it comes, it is a very pale and dead smile. It doesn't make you happy, you don't bubble up with it. It is not a radiance around you.

> Your whole mechanism is topsy-turvy because when you wanted to be angry you weren't; when you wanted to hate you didn't. Now you want to love, suddenly you find that the mechanism doesn't function.

When you want to be angry, be angry. Nothing is wrong in being angry. If you want to laugh, laugh. Nothing is wrong in laughing loudly. By and by you will see that your whole system is functioning. When it functions, really, it has a hum around it. Just like a car hums when everything is going well—the driver who loves the car knows that now everything is functioning well. There is an organic unity; the mechanism is functioning well.

You can see it—whenever a person's mechanism is functioning well you can sense the hum around him. He walks, but his step has a dance in it. He talks, but his words carry a subtle poetry in them. He looks at you, and he really looks; it is not just lukewarm, it is really warm. When he touches you, he really touches you; you can feel his energy moving into your body, a current of life being transferred . . . because his mechanism is functioning well.

Don't wear masks; otherwise you will create dysfunctions, blocks in your mechanism. There are many blocks in your body. A person who has been suppressing anger—his jaw becomes blocked. All the anger comes up to the jaw and then stops there. His hands become ugly; they don't have the graceful movement of a dancer, no, because the anger comes into the fingers and becomes blocked. Remember, anger has two outlets for release: one is the teeth, another is the fingers. All animals when they are angry will bite you with the teeth or they will start tearing you with the hands. So the nails and the teeth are the two points from where the anger is released.

I have a suspicion that wherever anger is suppressed too much, people have teeth trouble. Their teeth go wrong because too much energy is there and never released. And anybody who suppresses anger will eat more—angry people will always eat more because the teeth need some exercise. Angry people will smoke more. Angry people will talk more—they can become obsessive talkers because somehow the jaw needs exercise so that the energy is released a little bit. And angry people's hands will become knotted, ugly. If the energy had been released, they could have become beautiful hands.

If you suppress anything, there is some corresponding part in the body to the emotion. If you don't want to cry, your eyes will lose their luster because tears are needed; they are a very alive phenomenon. When once in a while you weep and cry—really you go into it, you become it, and tears start flowing from your eyes—your eyes are cleansed, your eyes become fresh again, young and virgin.

That's why women have more beautiful eyes—because they can still cry. Men have lost the beauty of their eyes because they have a wrong notion that men should not cry. If a small boy cries, even the parents say, "What are you doing? Are you being a sissy?" What nonsense! Because God has given you—man and woman—the same tear glands. If man were not meant to weep, there would have been no tear glands. Simple mathematics. Why do the tear glands exist in men in the same proportion as they exist in women? Eyes need weeping and crying, and it is really beautiful if you can cry and weep wholeheartedly.

Remember, if you cannot cry and weep wholeheartedly, you cannot laugh, either, because that is the other polarity. People who can laugh can also cry; people who cannot cry cannot laugh. And you may have observed it sometimes in children: if they laugh loudly and long, they start crying—because both things are joined. In the villages I have heard mothers saying to their children, "Don't laugh too much; otherwise you will start crying." Really true because the phenomena are not different, just the same energy moves to the opposite poles. So the second thing: Don't use masks—be true whatsoever the cost.

And the third thing about authenticity: Always remain in the present because all falseness enters either from the past or from the future. That which has passed has passed. Don't bother about it and don't carry it as a burden; otherwise, it will not allow you to be authentic to the

> That which has passed has passed. Don't bother about it and don't carry it as a burden, otherwise, it will not allow you to be authentic to the present.

17

present. And all that has not come has not come yet. Don't unnecessarily be bothered about the future, otherwise that will come into the present and destroy it. Be true to the present, and then you will be authentic. To be here now is to be authentic. No past, no future—this moment, all. This moment the whole eternity.

These three things, and you attain truthfulness. Then whatsoever you say will be true. Ordinarily you think you have to be careful to say the truth; I'm not saying that. I am saying create authenticity, and whatsoever you say will be true.

TRUTH IS NOT SOMETHING LOGICAL. By truth I don't mean a conclusion arrived at by logical, rational methods. By truth I mean the authenticity of being, not imposing anything that you are not, just being that which you are at whatsoever the risk, never becoming a hypocrite. If you are sad, you are sad. That is the truth in that moment; don't hide it. Don't put a false smile on your face because that false smile will create a split in you. You will become two—a part of you will be smiling, and of course it is only going to be a minor part, and the major part will remain sad. Now a division has arisen, and if you go on doing it again and again . . .

When you are angry, you don't show your anger—you are afraid it may destroy your image because people think you are so compassionate, and people say that you are never angry. They appreciate it, and it is so gratifying to the ego. Now, being angry will destroy your beautiful image, so rather than destroying the image, you repress the anger. It is boiling within, but on the surface you remain compassionate, kind, polite, sweet. Now the division is being practiced. People are practicing it through their whole lives; then the division becomes absolutely settled. Even when you are sitting alone and there is nobody, and there is no need to pretend, you go on pretending; it has become second nature. People are not true even in their bathrooms; even when they are utterly alone, they are untrue. Now it is not a question of being true or untrue; it has just become their habit. For the whole of their lives they have practiced, and as you practice more and more, the distance between the two parts of you becomes bigger and bigger.

When it becomes unbridgeable, we call it schizophrenia. When you cannot contact your own other part, you almost become two persons instead of one; then it is severe mental illness. But everybody is divided, so the difference between the schizophrenic and the normal is only of degree. It is not very basic, not of quality but only of quantity.

By truth I mean not to pretend. Just be whatsoever you are—one moment you are sad, so that moment you are sad. And next moment if you become happy, there is no need now to continue to remain sad—because that, too, has been taught: to always be consistent, to remain consistent. It happens, you can observe it—you were sad, and then suddenly sadness is gone, but you cannot laugh immediately because what will people think? Are you mad? Just before you were sad; now you immediately start laughing? Only mad people or small children do this; it is not expected of you. You will have to wait for a certain situation in which slowly, slowly you can relax and start smiling and laughing again.

So it is not only that when you are sad you pretend smiles; when

> Even when you are sitting alone and there is nobody, and there is no need to pretend, you go on pretending; it has become second nature. People are not true even in their bathrooms; even when they are utterly alone, they are untrue.

you want to smile then, too, you pretend sadness because of that whole stupid idea of remaining consistent. Each moment has its own way, and no moment needs to be consistent with any other moment. Life is a flux, it is a river: It goes on changing its moods. So one need not be worried about consistency. Anybody who becomes worried about consistency will become untrue because only lies can be consistent. Truth is always changing. Truth contains its own contradictions—and that's the richness of truth, that's its vastness, that's its beauty.

So if you are feeling sad, then be sad—with no condemnation, with no evaluation of it being good or bad. There is no question of good or bad, it is simply so. And when it goes, let it go. When again you start smiling, don't feel guilty because just now you were sad, so how can you smile? Let somebody first tell a joke, let somebody first break the ice, and then you will smile. Wait for the right moment. That is again hypocrisy. When you are happy, be happy; there is no need to pretend anything.

> If you have an ideal, you cannot be true to the moment because the ideal is always there and you have to imitate the ideal. The true man has no ideals.

And remember: Each moment has an atomic reality. It is discontinuous from the past moment and it is not connected with the future moment. Each moment is atomic. They are not following each other in a sequence, they are not linear. Each moment has its own way of being, and you have to be that, in that moment, nothing else. This is what is really meant by truth.

Truth means authenticity, truth means sincerity. Truth is not a logical thing. It is a psychological state of being true—not true according to some ideal, because if there is some ideal you will become false. If you think that to be like a Buddha is to be true, then you will never be true because you are *not* a Buddha, and you will impose the Buddha on you. You can sit like the Buddha, you can almost become a marble statue, but deep down you will still be the same. The Buddha will be just a posture. And if you have an ideal, you cannot be true to the moment because the ideal is always there and you have to imitate the ideal.

The true man has no ideals. He lives moment to moment; he always lives as he feels in the moment. He is utterly respectful toward his feelings, his emotions, his moods. And this is what I want people to be: authentic, true, sincere, respectful toward their own soul.

LISTEN TO YOURSELF

Always listen to your own feelings, there is no need to look around. And by looking at people, you cannot see exactly what is happening to them because their face is not their reality, just as your face is not your reality. Their outside appearance is not their inner, just as your outside appearance is not your inner.

That is the whole hypocrisy of society—not to show your inner, your center, your real face. Hide it. Show it only to someone who is very intimate and who will understand. But who is intimate? Even lovers don't show their faces to each other. Because nobody knows; this minute somebody is a

> Don't look at others, look at yourself. And let what is inside of you come out, whatsoever the risk. There is no greater risk than suppression.

lover, next minute maybe not. So each becomes like an island, closed.

Don't look at others, look at yourself. And let what is inside of you come out, whatsoever the risk. There is no greater risk than suppression. If you suppress, you will lose all zest for life, all enthusiasm. You will lose all life if you go on suppressing. It is toxic; it poisons the being.

> Once you know how to be true, it is so beautiful that you will never settle for being false. We go on deciding to be false because we have never tasted the real.

Listen to the heart, and whatsoever is there, bring it out. Soon you will become efficient in bringing it out, and you will enjoy it. And once you know how to be true, it is so beautiful that you will never settle for being false. We go on deciding to be false because we have never tasted the real. From the very beginning of childhood the real was suppressed. Before a child becomes aware of what is real, he has been taught to suppress it. In unconscious ways, mechanical ways, he goes on suppressing without knowing what he is doing.

Be true to yourself—there is no other responsibility. One has to be responsible toward one's being. You are answerable to your own being, and God is not going to ask you why you were not somebody else.

There is a story that when the Hasid mystic Josiah was dying, somebody asked him why wasn't he praying to God, and was he sure that Moses would be a witness to him. He replied, "Let me tell you one thing. God is not going to ask me why I am not a Moses. He will ask me why I am not a Josiah."

This is the whole problem, how to be oneself. And if you can solve this, then every other problem becomes nonproblematic. Then life is a beautiful mystery to be lived—not a problem to be solved but just to be lived and enjoyed.

TRUST YOURSELF

Trust is possible only if first you trust in yourself. The most fundamental thing has to happen within you first. If you trust in yourself, you can trust in me, you can trust in people, you can trust in existence. But if you don't trust in yourself, then no other trust is ever possible.

And society destroys trust at the very roots. It does not allow you to trust yourself. It teaches all other kinds of trust—trust in the parents, trust in the church, trust in the state, trust in God, ad infinitum—but the basic trust is completely destroyed. And then all other trusts are phony, are bound to be phony. Then all other trusts are just plastic flowers. You don't have real roots for real flowers to grow.

Society does it deliberately, on purpose, because a man who trusts in himself is dangerous for society—a society that depends on slavery, a society that has invested too much in slavery. A man trusting himself is an independent man. You cannot make predictions about him, he will move in his own way. Freedom will be his life. He will trust when he feels, when he loves, and then his trust will have a tremendous intensity and truth in it. Then his trust will be alive and authentic. And he will be ready to risk all for his trust—but only when he feels it, only when it is true, only when it stirs his heart, only when it stirs his intelligence and his love. Otherwise not. You cannot force him into any kind of believing.

This society depends on belief. Its whole structure is that of auto-

> This earth, this beautiful earth, we have turned into a great prison. A few power-lusty people have reduced the whole of humanity into a mob. Man is allowed to exist only if he compromises with all kinds of nonsense.

hypnosis. Its whole structure is based in creating robots and machines, not men. It needs dependent people—so much so that they are constantly in need of being tyrannized, so much so that they are searching and seeking their own tyrants, their own Adolf Hitlers, their own Mussolinis, their own Josef Stalins and Mao Ze-dongs. This earth, this beautiful earth, we have turned into a great prison. A few power-lusty people have reduced the whole of humanity into a mob. Man is allowed to exist only if he compromises with all kinds of nonsense.

Now, to tell a child to believe in God is nonsense, utter nonsense—not that God does not exist, but because the child has not yet felt the thirst, the desire, the longing. He is not yet ready to go in search of the truth, the ultimate truth of life. He is not yet mature enough to inquire into the reality of existence. That love affair has to happen someday, but it can happen only if no belief is imposed upon him. If he is converted before the thirst has arisen to explore and to know, then his whole life he will live in a phony way; he will live in a pseudo way.

Yes, he will talk about God because he has been told that God is. He has been told authoritatively, and he has been told by people who were very powerful in his childhood—his parents, his priests, his teachers. He has been told by people, and he had to accept it; it was a question of his survival. He could not say no to his parents because without them he would not be able to live at all. It was too risky to say no; he had to say yes. But his yes can't be true.

How can it be true? He is saying yes only as a political device, to survive. You have not turned him into a religious person, you have made him a diplomat, you have created a politician. You have sabotaged his potential to grow into an authentic being. You have poisoned him. You have destroyed the very possibility of his intelligence because intelligence arises only when the longing arises to know. Now the longing will never arise because before the question has taken possession of his soul, the answer has already been supplied. Before he was hungry, the food has been forced into his being. Now, without hunger, this forced food cannot be digested; there is no hunger to digest it. That's why people live like pipes through which life passes like undigested food.

One has to be very patient with children, very alert, very conscious not to say anything that may hinder their own intelligence from arriving, not to convert them into Christians, Hindus, and Muhammadans. One needs infinite patience. One day that miracle happens, when the child himself starts inquiring. Then, too, don't supply him with ready-made answers. Ready-made answers help nobody; ready-made answers are dull and stupid. Help him to become more intelligent. Rather than giving him answers, give him situations and chal-

> One has to be very patient with children, very alert, very conscious not to say anything that may hinder their own intelligence from arriving.

lenges so that his intelligence is sharpened and he asks more deeply—so that the question penetrates to his very core, so that the question becomes a question of life and death.

But that is not allowed. Parents are very much afraid, society is very much afraid. If children are allowed to remain free, who knows? They may never come to the fold the parents belonged to, they may never go to the church—Catholic, Protestant, this or that. Who knows what is going to happen when they become intelligent on their own? They will not be within your control. And this society goes into deeper and deeper politics to control everybody, to possess everybody's soul.

That's why the first thing they have to do is to destroy trust—the trust of the child in himself, the confidence of the child in himself. They have to make him shaky and afraid. Once he is trembling, he is controllable. If he is confident, he is uncontrollable. If he is confident he will assert himself, he will try to do his own thing. He will never want to do anybody else's thing. He will go on his own journey, he will not fulfill somebody else's desires for some trip. He will never be an imitator, he will never be a dull and dead person. He will be so alive, so pulsating with life, that nobody will be able to control him.

Destroy his trust, and you have castrated him. You have taken his power; now he will always be powerless and always in need of somebody to dominate, direct, and command him. Now he will be a good soldier, a good citizen, a good nationalist, a good Christian, a good Mohammedan, a good Hindu.

Yes, he will be all these things. But he will not be a real individual. He will not have any roots, he will be uprooted his whole life. He will live without roots—and to live without roots is to live in misery, is to live in hell. Just as trees need roots in the earth, man is also a tree and needs roots in existence or else he will live a very un-intelligent life.

Just the other day, I was reading a story:

Three surgeons, old friends, met on holiday. On the beach, sitting under the sun, they started boasting. The first said, "I came across a man who had lost both of his legs in the war. I gave him artificial legs, and it has been a miracle. Now he has become one of the greatest runners in the world! There is every possibility that in the coming Olympics, he will win."

The other said, "That's nothing. I came across a woman who fell from a thirty-story building. Her face was completely crushed. I did a great job of plastic surgery. Just the other day I came to know through the newspapers that she has become the world beauty queen."

The third was a humble man. The others looked at him and asked, "What have you done lately? What's new?"

The man said, "Nothing much—and moreover, I am not allowed to say anything about it."

His colleagues became more curious. They said, "But we are friends, we can keep your secret. You need not be worried; it won't leak out."

So he said, "Okay, if you say so, if you promise: A man was brought to me, he had lost his head in a car accident. I was at a loss to know what to do. I rushed into my garden just to think what to do, and suddenly I came across a cabbage. Finding nothing else, I transplanted the cabbage in place of the head. And do you know what? That man has become the president of the United States."

> The unintelligent
> person is easily
> understood. He fits
> with the gestalt of
> society, the society
> has values and
> criteria by which
> to judge him. But
> it takes years for
> society to evaluate
> a genius.

You can destroy the child; still, he can become the president of the United States. There is no inherent impossibility of becoming successful without intelligence. In fact, it is more difficult to become successful *with* intelligence because the intelligent person is inventive. He is always ahead of his time; it takes time to understand him.

The unintelligent person is easily understood. He fits with the gestalt of society; the society has values and criteria by which to judge him. But it takes years for society to evaluate a genius.

I am not saying that a person who has no intelligence cannot become successful, cannot become famous—but he will still remain phony. And that is the misery: You can become famous, but if you are phony, you live in misery. You don't know what blessings life is showering on you—you will never know. You don't have enough intelligence to know. You will never see the beauty of existence because you don't have the sensitivity to know it. You will never see the sheer miracle that surrounds you, that crosses your path in millions of ways every day. You will never see it because to see it, you need a tremendous capacity to understand, to feel, to be.

This society is a power-oriented society. This society is still utterly primitive, utterly barbarian. A few people—politicians, priests, professors—are dominating millions. And this society is run in such a way that no child is allowed to have intelligence. It is a sheer accident that once in a while a Buddha arrives on the earth—a sheer accident. Somehow, once in a while a person escapes from the clutches of society. Once in a while a person remains unpoisoned by society. That must be because of some error, some mistake of society. Otherwise society succeeds in destroying your roots, in destroying your trust in yourself. And once that is done, you will never be able to trust anybody. Once you are incapable of loving yourself, you will never be able to love anybody. That is an absolute truth, there are no exceptions to it. You can love others only if you are able to

> It is a sheer accident that once in a while a Buddha arrives on the earth—a sheer accident. Somehow, once in a while a person escapes from the clutches of society.

love yourself. But society condemns self-love. It says it is selfishness, it says it is narcissistic.

Yes, self-love can become narcissistic, but it is not necessarily so. It can become narcissistic if it never moves beyond itself, it can become a kind of selfishness if it becomes confined to oneself. Otherwise, self-love is the beginning of all other loves.

A person who loves himself sooner or later starts overflowing with love. A person who trusts himself cannot distrust anybody, even those who are going to deceive him, even those who have already deceived him. Yes, he cannot even distrust them because now he knows trust is far more valuable than anything else.

You can cheat a person—but of what can you cheat him? You can take some money or something else from him. But the man who knows the beauty of trust will not be distracted by these small things. He will still love you, he will still trust you. And then a miracle hap-

> Once you are
> incapable of loving
> yourself, you will
> never be able to love
> anybody. That is an
> absolute truth, there
> are no exceptions
> to it.

pens: If a person really trusts you, it is impossible to cheat him, almost impossible.

It happens every day in your life, too. Whenever you trust somebody, it becomes impossible for him to cheat you, to deceive you. Sitting on the platform in a railway station, you don't know the person who is sitting by your side—he is a stranger, a complete stranger—and you say to him, "Please just watch my luggage. I have to go to purchase a ticket." And you go. You trust an absolute stranger. But it almost never happens that the stranger deceives you. He could have deceived you if you had not trusted him.

Trust has a magic in it. How can he deceive you now that you have trusted him? How can he fall so low? He will never be able to forgive himself if he deceives you.

There is an intrinsic quality in human consciousness to trust and to be trusted. Everybody enjoys being trusted. It is respect from the other person—and when you trust a stranger it is more so. There is no reason to trust him, and still you trust him. You raise the man to such a high pedestal, you value the man so much, it is almost impossible for him to fall from that height. And if he falls, he will never be able to forgive himself, he will have to carry the weight of guilt his whole life.

A man who trusts himself comes to know the beauty of it—comes to know that the more you trust yourself, the more you bloom; the more you are in a state of let-go and relaxation, the more you are settled and serene, the more you are calm, cool, and quiet. And it is so beautiful that you start trusting more and more people because the more you trust, the more your calmness deepens; your coolness goes deeper and deeper to the very core of your being. And the more you trust, the more you soar high. A man who can trust will sooner or later know the logic of trust. And then one day he is bound to try to trust the unknown.

> ☙
>
> **If a person really trusts you, it is impossible to cheat him, almost impossible.**

Start trusting yourself—that is the fundamental lesson, the first lesson. Start loving yourself. If you don't love yourself, who else is going to love you? But remember, if you *only* love yourself, your love will be very poor.

A great Jewish mystic, Hillel, has said, "If you are not for yourself, who is going to be for you?" And also, "If you are only for yourself, then what meaning can your life ever have?"—a tremendously significant statement. Remember it: Love yourself because if you don't love yourself, nobody else will ever be able to love you.

You cannot love a person who hates himself. And on this unfortunate earth, almost everybody hates himself, everybody condemns himself. How can you love a person who is condemnatory toward himself? He will not believe you. He cannot love himself—how can *you* dare? He cannot love himself—how can *you* love him? He will suspect some game, some trick, some trip. He will suspect that you are trying to deceive him in the name of love. He will be very cautious, alert, and his suspicion will poison your being. If you love a person who hates himself, you are trying to destroy his concept about himself. And nobody easily drops his concept about himself; that is his

How can you love a person who is condemnatory toward himself? He will not believe you. He cannot love himself— how can you dare?

identity. He will fight with you, he will prove to you that he is right and you are wrong.

That's what is happening in every love relationship—let me call it every so-called love relationship. It is happening between every husband and wife, every lover and beloved, every man and every woman. How can you destroy the other's concept about himself? That is his identity, that is his ego, that's how he knows himself. If you take it away, he will not know who he is. It is too risky; he cannot drop his concept so easily. He will prove to you that he is not worth loving; he is only worth hating. And the same is the case with you. You also hate yourself; you cannot allow anybody else to love you. Whenever somebody comes with loving energy around you, you shrink, you want to escape, you are afraid. You know perfectly well that you are unworthy of love, you know that only on the surface do you look so good, so beautiful; deep down you are ugly. And if you allow this person to love you, sooner or later—and it will be sooner rather than later—he will come to know who you are in reality.

How long will you be able to pretend with a person with whom you have to live in love? You can pretend in the marketplace, you can pretend in the Lions Club and the Rotary Club—smiles, all smiles. You can do beautiful acting and role-playing. But if you live with a woman or a man for twenty-four hours a day, then it is tiring to go on smiling and smiling and smiling. Then the smile tires you because it is phony. It is just an exercise of the lips, and the lips become tired.

How can you go on being sweet? Your bitterness will surface. Hence, by the time the honeymoon is over, everything is over. Both have known each other's reality, both have known each other's phoniness, both have known each other's falsity.

> *Without you this universe will lose some poetry, some beauty: A song will be missed, a note will be missed, there will be a gap—nobody has told you that.*

One is afraid to become intimate. To be intimate means you will have to put aside the role. And you know who you are: worthless, just dirt; that's what you have been told from the very beginning. Your parents, your teachers, your priests, your politicians—all have been telling you that you are dirt, worthless. Nobody has ever accepted you. Nobody has given you the feeling that you are loved and respected, that you are needed—that this existence will miss you, that without you this existence will not be the same, that without you there will be a hole. Without you this universe will lose some poetry, some beauty: A song will be missed, a note will be missed, there will be a gap—nobody has told you that.

And that's what my work here is: to destroy the distrust that has been created in you about yourself, to destroy all condemnation that has been imposed on you, to take it away from you and to give you a feeling that you are loved and respected, <u>loved by existence</u>. God has created you because he loved you. He loved you so much that he could not resist the temptation to create you.

When a painter paints, he paints because he loves. Vincent van Gogh continually painted the sun his whole life, he loved the sun so much. In fact, it was the sun that drove him mad. For one year continuously he was standing and painting under the hot sun. His whole life revolved around the sun. And the day he was contented, painting the painting that he had always wanted to paint—and to paint this painting he had painted many others, but he had not been contented with them—the day he was contented, the day he could say, "Yes, this is the thing that I wanted to paint," he committed suicide because, he said, "My work is done. I have done the thing that I came for. My destiny is fulfilled, now it is pointless to live."

His whole life a devotion to a certain painting? He must have been madly in love with the sun. He looked at the sun so long that it destroyed his eyes, his vision, it drove him mad.

When a poet composes a song, it is because he loves it. God has painted you, sung you, danced you. God loves you! If you don't see any meaning in the word *God,* don't be worried. Call it existence, call it the whole. The existence loves you, otherwise you would not be here.

Relax into your being, you are cherished by the whole. That's why the whole goes on breathing in you, pulsating in you. Once you start feeling this tremendous respect and love and trust of the whole in you, you will start growing roots into your being. You will trust yourself. And only then can you trust me, only then can you trust your friends, your children, your husband, your wife. Only then can you trust the trees and the animals and the stars and the moon. Then one simply lives as trust. It is no more a question of trusting this or that; one simply trusts. And to trust is simply to be religious.

That's what *sannyas* is all about. *Sannyas* is to undo all that society has done. It is not just accidental that priests are against me, politicians are against me, parents are against me, the whole establishment is against me; it is not accidental. I can understand the absolutely clear logic of it. I am trying to undo what they have done. I am sabotaging the whole pattern of this slave society.

My effort is to create rebels, and the beginning of the rebel is to trust in oneself. If I can help you to trust in yourself, I have helped you. Nothing else is needed; everything else follows of its own accord.

INTIMACY WITH OTHERS
THE NEXT STEPS

When two lovers are really open to each other, when they are not afraid of each other and not hiding anything from each other, that is intimacy. When they can say each and everything without any fear that the other will be offended or hurt. . . . If the lover thinks the other will be offended, then the intimacy is not yet deep enough. Then it is a kind of arrangement, which can be broken by anything. But when two lovers start feeling that there is nothing to hide and everything can be said, and the trust has come to such a depth where even if you don't say it the other is going to know, then they start becoming one.

BE SEEN

Life is a pilgrimage, and unless love is attained, it remains a pilgrimage, never reaching anywhere. It goes on moving in circles, and the moment of fulfillment never comes when one can say, "I have arrived. I have become that for which I had come. The seed is fulfilled in the flowers." Love is the goal, life is the journey. And a journey without a goal is bound to be neurotic, haphazard; it will not have any direction. One day you are going north, and another day you are going south; it will remain accidental, anything can lead you anywhere. You will remain driftwood unless the goal is clear. It may be a very distant star—that doesn't make any difference—but it should be clear. If it is distant, it is okay, but it should be there.

Your eyes can remain focused on it; then the journey of ten thousand miles is not a long journey. If you are moving in the right direction, then the longest journey is not such a problem. But if you are moving in a wrong direction, or not moving in any direction at all, or moving in all directions together, then life starts collapsing. That's what neurosis is—a collapse in energy, not knowing where to go, what to do, what to be. Not knowing where to go, not knowing what it is all about, leaves a gap inside, a wound, a dark hole, and constant fear will arise out of it. That's why people live in trembling. They may hide it, they may cover it up, they may not show it to anybody, but they live in fear. That's why people are so afraid of being intimate with somebody—the other may see the black hole inside you if you allow them too close an intimacy.

The word *intimacy* comes from the Latin root *intimum,* which means your interiority, your innermost core. Unless you have something there, you can't be intimate with anybody. You cannot allow *intimum,* intimacy, because they will see the hole, the wound, and the pus oozing out of it. They will see that you don't know who you are, that you are a madman, that you don't know where you are going. That you have not even heard your own song, that your life is a chaos, not a cosmos. Hence the fear of intimacy.

Even lovers rarely become intimate. And just to be sexually related to somebody is not intimacy—the genital orgasm is not all that is there in intimacy, it is just the periphery of it. Intimacy can be with it or it can be without it. Intimacy is a totally different dimension. It is allowing the other to come into you, to see you as you see yourself—to

> Intimacy is a totally different dimension. It is allowing the other to come into you, to see you as you see yourself—to allow the other to see you from your inside, to invite somebody to that deepest core of your being.

allow the other to see you from your inside, to invite somebody to that deepest core of your being. In the modern world intimacy is disappearing. Even lovers are not intimate. Friendship is only a word now; it has disappeared. And the reason? The reason is that there is nothing to share. Who wants to show one's inner poverty? One wants to pretend, "I am rich, I have arrived, I know what I am doing, I know where I am going."

One is not ready and courageous enough to open up, to show one's inner chaos and be vulnerable. The other may exploit it; that fear is there. The other may become too dominant, seeing that you are a chaos. Seeing that you need a master, that you are not a master of your own being, the other may become the master. Hence, everybody tries to protect themselves so that nobody knows their inner helplessness; otherwise they can be exploited. This world consists of much exploitation.

Love is the goal. And once the goal is clear, you start growing an inner richness. The wound disappears and becomes a lotus; the wound is transformed into a lotus. That is the miracle of love, the magic of love. Love is the greatest alchemical force in the world. Those who know how to use it can reach the highest peak called God. Those who know not how to use it remain crawling in the dark recesses of existence; they never come to the sunlit peaks of life.

THE NEED FOR PRIVACY

The being has two sides, the without and the within. The without can be public, but the within cannot be. If you make the within public, you will lose your soul, you will lose your original face. Then you will live as if you have no inner being. Life will become drab, futile. It happens to people who lead a public life—politicians, film actors. They become public, they lose their inner being completely; they don't know who they are except what the public says about them. They depend on others' opinions; they don't have a sense of their being.

One of the most famous actresses, Marilyn Monroe, committed suicide, and psychoanalysts have been brooding on the reason why. She was one of the most beautiful women ever, one of the most successful. Even the president of the United States, John F. Kennedy, was in love with her, and millions of people loved her. One cannot think of what more you can have. She had everything.

But she was public and she knew it. Even in her love chamber when President Kennedy would be there, she addressed him as "Mr. President"—as if one was making love not to a man but to an institution.

She was an institution. By and by she became aware that she had nothing private. Once she had just posed for a nude calendar, and somebody asked, "Did you have anything on while you posed for the calendar?"

She replied, "Yes, I had something on—the radio."

Exposed, nude, no private self. My feeling is that she committed suicide because that was the only thing left she could have done privately. Everything was public; that was the only thing left she could

> ⤞
>
> My feeling is that Marilyn Monroe committed suicide because that was the only thing left she could have done privately. Everything was public; that was the only thing left she could do on her own.

do on her own, alone, something absolutely intimate and secret. Public figures are always tempted toward suicide because only through suicide can they have a glimpse of who they are.

All that is beautiful is inner, and the inner means privacy. Have you watched women making love? They always close their eyes. They know something. A man goes on making love with open eyes; he remains a watcher. He is not completely in the act; he is not totally in it. He remains a voyeur, as if somebody else is making love and he is watching, as if the lovemaking is on a TV screen or in a movie. But a woman knows better because she is more delicately tuned to the inner. She always closes her eyes. Then love has a totally different fragrance.

Do one thing: At night run the bath, and then switch on and off the light. When there is darkness you will hear the water falling more clearly, the sound will be sharp. When the light is on, the sound will be not so sharp. What happens in darkness? In darkness, because you cannot see, everything else disappears. Only you and the sound are there. That's why in all good restaurants sharp light is avoided. They are candlelit. Whenever a restaurant is candlelit, taste is deeper—you eat well and you taste more. The fragrance surrounds you. If there is very bright light, the taste is no longer there. The eyes make everything public.

In the very first sentence of his *Metaphysics,* Aristotle says that sight is the highest sense of man. It is not—in fact, sight has become too domineering. It has monopolized the whole self and destroyed all the other senses. Aristotle's master, Plato, says that there is a hierarchy in the senses—sight at the top, touch at the bottom. He is absolutely wrong. There is no hierarchy. All senses are on the same level, and there should not be any hierarchy.

But you live through the eyes: Eighty percent of your life is eye oriented. This should not be so; a balance has to be restored. You should also touch, because touch has something that eyes cannot give. But try, *try* to touch the woman you love or the man you love in bright light, and then touch in darkness. In darkness the body reveals itself; in bright light it hides.

Have you seen Renoir's paintings of feminine bodies? They have something miraculous in them. Many painters have painted the feminine body, but there is no comparison with Renoir. What is the difference? All other painters have painted the feminine body as it looks to the eyes. Renoir has painted it as it feels to the hands, so the paintings have a warmth and a closeness, an aliveness.

> Eighty percent of your life is eye oriented. This should not be so, a balance has to be restored. You should also touch, because touch has something that eyes cannot give.

When you touch, something happens very close. When you see, something is far away. In darkness, in secrecy, in privacy, something is revealed that cannot be revealed in openness, in the marketplace. Others are seeing and observing; something deep within you shrinks, it cannot flower. It is just as if you put seeds down on the open ground for everybody to look at. They will never sprout. They need to be thrown deep in the womb of the earth, in deep darkness where nobody can see them. There they start sprouting, and a great tree is born.

> Just as seeds need darkness and privacy in the earth, all relationships that are deep and intimate remain inner. They need privacy, they need a place where only two exist.

Just as seeds need darkness and privacy in the earth, all relationships that are deep and intimate remain inner. They need privacy, they need a place where only two exist. Then a moment comes when even the two dissolve, and only one exists.

Two lovers deeply in tune with each other dissolve. Only one exists. They breathe together, they are together; a togetherness exists. This would not be possible if observers were there. They would never be able to let go if others were watching. The very eyes of others would become the barrier. So all that is beautiful, all that is deep, happens in darkness.

In human relationships, privacy is needed. Secrecy has its own reason to be there. Remember that, and always remember that you will behave very foolishly in life if you become completely public. It will be as if somebody has turned his pockets inside out. That will be your shape, like pockets turned inside out. Nothing is wrong in being outward, but remember, that is only part of life. It should not become the whole.

I am not saying to move in darkness forever. Light has its own beauty and its own reason. If the seed remains in the dark forever and ever, and never comes up to receive the sun in the morning, it will be dead. It has to go into darkness to sprout, to gather strength, to become vital, to be reborn; and then it has to come out and face the world and the light and the storm and the rains. It has to accept the challenge of the outside. But that challenge can only be accepted if you are deeply rooted within.

I am not saying to become escapists. I am not saying to close your eyes, move within and never come out. I am simply saying go in so that you can come out with energy, with love, with compassion. Go in so that when you come out you are not a beggar but a king. Go in so that when you come out you have something to share—the flowers, the leaves. Go in so that your coming out becomes richer and is not impoverished. And always remember whenever you feel exhausted that the source of energy is within. Close your eyes and go in.

Make outer relationships, and make inner relationships also. Of course there are bound to be outer relationships—you move in the world, business relationships will be there—but they should not be all. They have their part to play, but there must be something absolutely secret and private, something that you can call your own.

That is what Marilyn Monroe lacked. She was a public woman, successful, yet completely a failure. While she was at the top of her success and fame, she committed suicide. Why she committed suicide has remained an enigma. She had everything to live for; you cannot conceive of more fame, more success, more charisma, more beauty, more health. Everything was there, nothing could be improved upon, and still something was lacking. The inside, the within, was empty. Then, suicide is the only way.

You may not be daring enough to commit suicide like Marilyn Monroe. You may be very cowardly and commit suicide very slowly—you may take seventy years to commit it—but still it will be a suicide. Unless you have something inside you that is not dependent on anything outside, that is just your own—a world, a space of your own where you can close your eyes and move, and you can forget that anything else exists—you will be committing suicide.

> I will not say that your life should be an open book, no. A few chapters open, okay. And a few chapters completely closed, a complete mystery.

Life arises from that inner source and spreads into the sky outside. There has to be a balance—I am always for balance. So I will not say that your life should be an open book, no. A few chapters open, okay. And a few chapters completely closed, a complete mystery. If you are just an open book you will be a prostitute, you will just be standing in the marketplace naked, with just the radio on. No, that won't do.

If your whole book is open, you will be just the day with no night, just the summer with no winter. Where will you rest, and where will you center yourself, and where will you take refuge? Where will you move when the world is too much? Where will you go to pray and meditate? No, half and half is perfect. Let half of your book be open—open to everybody, available to everybody—and let the other half of your book be so secret that only rare guests are allowed there.

Only rarely is somebody allowed to move within your temple. That is how it should be. If the crowd is coming in and going out, then the temple is no longer a temple. It may be a waiting room in an airport, but it cannot be a temple. Only rarely, very rarely, do you allow somebody to enter your self. That is what love is.

WE HAVE ALWAYS LIVED WITH OTHERS. From the moment the child leaves the mother's womb, he is never alone—he is with the mother, with the family, with friends, with other people. The circle of acquaintances, friendships, relationships, becomes bigger and bigger, and a crowd gathers around him. That's what we call life. And the more people are there in your life, the more you think you have a rich life.

When you start moving inward, all those faces fade away, all that crowd disperses. You have to say good-bye to everybody: Even to your closest friend, your lover, you have to say good-bye. A moment comes where even your lover cannot be with you. That is the moment when you are again entering the same space as you were in the womb of the mother. But then you were not acquainted with the crowd, so you never felt alone. The child was perfectly happy in the mother's womb because there was no comparison, all was joy. Because he never knew the other, he could not feel lonely or alone—he had no idea. That was the only reality that he knew.

But now you have known the crowd, relationships, the joys and miseries of relationship, and both are there. Moving again inward, the world starts disappearing, becomes like an echo, and soon even the echo disappears and one is utterly lost. But this is just an interpretation. If you can go in a little bit more, suddenly you will find yourself— and for the first time you will find yourself. Then you will be surprised: You were lost in the crowd; now you are not lost. You were lost in that jungle of relationship, and now you have come home. Then again you can come back into the world, but you will be a totally different person.

You will relate, but you will not depend; you will love, but your love will not be a need. You will love, but you will not possess; you will love, but you will not be jealous. And when love is without jealousy, without possessiveness, it is divine. You will be with people. In fact, only then can you be with people because you *are;* now you can be with people. First you were not, so the whole idea of being with people was just illusory, a kind of dream.

Unless you *are,* how can you relate? Unless you *are,* how can you be with the other? It is just a fiction that we create; it is a delusion.

> Unless you are centered, unless you know who you are, you cannot really relate. The relationship that goes on without self-knowledge is just an illusion.

Unless you are centered, unless you know who you are, you cannot really relate. The relationship that goes on without self-knowledge is just an illusion. The other thinks he is relating to you, you think you are relating to him; neither do you know yourself nor does he know himself. So who is relating to whom? There is nobody! Just two shadows playing a game. And since both are shadows, there is no substance in the relationship. That's what I observe continuously: People relate, but there is nothing substantial. They relate because they are afraid that if they don't relate, they will fall into loneliness and feel lost, so they jump again and start relating. Any kind of relationship is better than no relationship; even if it is enmity it is okay; at least one feels occupied. Your so-called love is nothing but a kind of enmity, a polite way of fighting, struggling, nagging, dominating, a civilized way of torturing each other.

So you have to go into this space. Gather courage and go into it. Even if it feels very sad and very lonely, there is nothing to be worried about; we have to pay this price. And once you have reached your source, the whole thing will change completely, and you will come out of it as an individual. That is the difference I make between an individual and a person: A person is a false phenomenon, an individual is a reality. Persons, personalities, are masks, shadows; individuality is substance, it is reality. And only individuals can relate, can love—persons can only play games.

RELATING, NOT RELATIONSHIP

Love is a state of your consciousness when you are joyous, when there is a dance in your being. Something starts vibrating, radiating, from your center; something starts pulsating around you. It starts reaching people: it can reach women, it can reach men, it can reach rocks and trees and stars.

When I am talking about love, I am talking about this love: a love that is not a relationship but a state of being. Always remember: Whenever I use the word *love,* I use it as a state of being, not as a relationship. Relationship is only a very minor aspect of it. But your idea of love is basically that of relationship, as if that is all.

Relationship is needed only because you can't be alone, because you are not yet capable of meditation. Hence, meditation is a must before you can really love. One should be capable of being alone, utterly alone, and yet tremendously blissful. Then you can love. Then your love is no longer a need but a sharing, no longer a necessity. You will not become dependent on the people you love. You will share— and sharing is beautiful.

> Relationship is needed only because you can't be alone, because you are not yet capable of meditation. Hence, meditation is a must before you can really love.

But what ordinarily happens in the world is: You don't have love; the person you think you love has no love in his being, either, and both are asking for love from each other. Two beggars begging each other! Hence, the fight, the conflict, the continuous quarrel between the lovers—over trivia, over immaterial things, over stupid things!—but they go on quarreling.

The basic quarrel is that the husband thinks he is not getting what is his right to get; the wife thinks she is not getting what is her right to get. The wife thinks she has been deceived, and the husband also thinks that he has been deceived. Where is the love? Nobody bothers to give, everybody wants to get. And when everybody is after getting, nobody gets it and everybody feels at a loss, empty, tense.

The basic foundation is missing, and you have started making the temple without the foundation. It is going to fall and collapse any moment. And you know how many times your love has collapsed, and still you go on doing the same thing again and again.

> Sitting silently in your room and being so blissful, so blissed out? You must be crazy or something! People will suspect that you are on a drug, stoned.

You live in such unawareness! You don't see what you have been doing to your life and to others' lives. You go on mechanically, robotlike, repeating the old pattern, knowing perfectly well you have done this before. And you know what has always been the outcome, and deep down you are also alert that it is going to happen the same way again—because there is no difference. You are preparing for the same conclusion, the same collapse.

If you can learn anything from the failure of love, it is to become more aware, become more meditative. <u>And by meditation I mean the capacity to be joyous alone.</u> Very rare people are capable of being blissful for no reason at all—just sitting silently and blissfully! Others will think them mad because the idea of happiness is that it has to come from somebody else. You meet a beautiful woman and you are happy, or you meet a beautiful man and you are happy. But sitting silently in your room and being so blissful, so blissed out? You must be crazy or something! People will suspect that you are on a drug, stoned.

Yes, meditation is the ultimate LSD! It is releasing your own psychedelic powers. It is releasing your own imprisoned splendor. And you become so joyous, such a celebration arises in your being, that you need not have any relationship. Still you can relate with people . . . and that's the difference between relating and relationship.

Relationship is a thing: You cling to it. Relating is a flow, a movement, a process. You meet a person, you are loving because you have so much love to give— and the more you give, the more you have. Once you have understood this strange arithmetic of love—that the more you give, the more you have . . . This is just against the economic laws that operate in the outside world. Once you have known that, if you want to

> Relationship is a thing: You cling to it. Relating is a flow, a movement, a process. You meet a person, you are loving because you have so much love to give— and the more you give, the more you have.

have more love and more joy, you give and share, then you simply share. And whosoever allows you to share your joy with him or with her, you feel grateful to him or her. But it is not a relationship; it is a riverlike flow.

The river passes by the side of a tree, saying hello, nourishing the tree, giving water to the tree . . . and it moves on, dances on. It does not cling to the tree. And the tree does not say, "Where are you going? We are married! And before you can leave me you will need a divorce—at least a separation! Where are you going? And if you were going to leave me, why did you dance so beautifully around me? Why did you nourish me in the first place?" No, the tree showers its flowers onto the river in deep gratefulness, and the river moves on. The wind comes and dances around the tree and moves on. And the tree gives its fragrance to the wind.

This is relating. If humanity is ever going to become grown-up, mature, this will be the way of love: people meeting, sharing, moving, a nonpossessive quality, a nondominating quality. Otherwise love becomes a power trip.

TAKE THE RISK TO BE TRUE

No relationship can truly grow if you go on holding back. If you remain clever and go on safeguarding and protecting yourself, only personalities meet, and the essential centers remain alone. Then only your mask is related, not you. Whenever such a thing happens, there are four persons in the relationship, not two. Two false persons go on meeting, and the two real persons remain worlds apart.

Risk is there—if you become true, nobody knows whether this relationship will be capable of understanding truth, authenticity;

whether this relationship will be strong enough to stand in the storm. There is a risk, and because of it people remain very, very guarded. They say things that should be said, they do things that should be done; love becomes more or less like a duty. But then the reality remains hungry, and the essence is not fed. So the essence becomes sadder and sadder. The lies of the personality are a very heavy burden on the essence, on the soul. The risk is real, and there is no guarantee about it, but I will tell you that the risk is worth taking.

> ◈
>
> If you remain clever and go on safeguarding and protecting yourself, only personalities meet, and the essential centers remain alone. Then only your mask is related, not you.

At the most, the relationship can break—at the most. But it is better to be separate and real than unreal and together because then it is never going to be satisfying. Benediction will never come out of it. You will remain hungry and thirsty, and you will go on dragging, just waiting for some miracle to happen.

For the miracle to happen you will have to do something, and that is: Start being true. At the risk that maybe the relationship is not strong enough and may not be able to bear it—the truth may be too much, unbearable—but then that relationship is not worthwhile. So that test has to be passed.

Risk everything for truth; otherwise you will remain discontented. You will do many things, but nothing will really happen to you. You will move much, but you will never arrive anywhere. The whole effect will be almost absurd. It is as if you are hungry and you simply fantasize about food—beautiful, delicious. But fantasy is fantasy; it is not real. You cannot eat unreal food. For moments you can delude yourself,

> The lies of the personality are a very heavy burden on the essence, on the soul. The risk is real, and there is no guarantee about it, but I will tell you that the risk is worth taking.

you can live in a dreamlike world, but a dream is not going to give you anything. It will take many things from you, and it will not give you anything in return.

The time that you spend using a false personality is simply wasted; it will never come back to you again. Those same moments could have been real, authentic. Even a single moment of authenticity is better than a whole life of inauthentic living. So don't be afraid. The mind will say to you to go on safeguarding the other and yourself, to keep safe. That's how millions of people are living.

Freud in his last days wrote in a letter to a friend that as far as he had observed through his life—and he really observed deeply; nobody has observed so deeply, so penetratingly, so persistently and so scientifically—one conclusion seems absolutely certain: that people cannot live without lies. Truth is dangerous. Lies are very sweet but unreal. Delicious! You go on saying sweet nothings to your lover, and he goes on whispering in your ear sweet (but) nothings. And meanwhile life goes on slipping out of your hands, and everybody is coming closer and closer to death.

Before death comes, remember one thing: Love has to be lived before death happens. Otherwise you live in vain, and the whole of your life will be futile, a desert. Before death comes, make it a certainty that love has happened. But that is possible only with the truth. So be true. Risk everything for truth, and never risk truth for anything else. Let this be the fundamental law: Even if I have to sacrifice myself, my life, I am going to sacrifice it for truth, but truth I will never sacrifice for anything. And tremendous happiness will be yours, undreamed of benedictions will shower on you.

Once you are true, everything else becomes possible. If you are false—just a facade, a painted thing, a face, a mask—nothing is possible. Because with the false only the false happens, and with the truth, truth.

I understand the problem, the problem of all lovers, that deep down they are afraid. They go on wondering whether this relationship will be strong enough to bear truth. But how can you know beforehand? There is no a priori knowledge. One has to move into it to know it. How are you to know, sitting inside your house, whether you will be able to withstand the storm and the wind outside? You have never been in the storm. Go and see! Trial and error is the only way. Go and see—maybe you will be defeated, but even in that defeat you will have become stronger than you are right now.

> Lies are very sweet but unreal. Delicious! You go on saying sweet nothings to your lover, and he goes on whispering in your ear sweet (but) nothings.

If one experience defeats you, then another and another, by and by the very going through the storm will make you stronger and stronger and stronger. A day comes when one simply starts delighting in the storm, one simply starts dancing in the storm. Then the storm is not the enemy—that, too, is an opportunity, a wild opportunity, to *be.*

Remember, being never happens comfortably, otherwise it would have happened to all. Remember, being cannot happen conveniently, otherwise everybody would have being without any problem. Being

> The problem of all lovers is that deep down they are afraid. They go on wondering whether this relationship will be strong enough to bear truth. But how can you know beforehand?

happens only when you take risks, when you move in danger. And love is the greatest danger there is. It demands you totally.

So don't be afraid, go into it. If the relationship survives truth, it will be beautiful. If it dies, then, too, it is good because one false relationship has ended and now you will be more capable of moving into another relationship, truer, more solid, more concerning the essence.

But remember always, falsity never pays; it appears to, but it never pays. Only truth pays—and in the beginning truth never looks like it will pay. It seems it will shatter everything. If you look at it from the outside, truth looks very very dangerous, terrible. But this is an outside view. If you go in, truth is the only beautiful thing. And once you start cherishing it, tasting it, you will demand more and more because it will bring contentment.

Have you watched it? It's easier to be true with strangers. People traveling in a train start talking with strangers, and they assert things they have never asserted to their friends because with the stranger, nothing is involved. After half an hour your station will come, and you will get off; you will forget, and he will forget what you have said. So whatever you have said makes no difference. Nothing is at stake with a stranger.

People talking to strangers are truer, and they reveal their heart. But talking with friends, with relatives—father, mother, wife, husband,

brother, sister—there is a deep unconscious inhibition. "Don't say this, he may
feel hurt. Don't do that, she won't like
it. Don't behave in this way, Father is
old, he may be shocked." So one goes
on controlling. By and by, the truth is
dropped into the basement of your being, and you become very clever and
cunning with the untrue. You go on
smiling false smiles, which are just
painted on the lips. You go on saying
good things, meaning nothing. You are
getting bored with your boyfriend or

> If the relationship
> survives truth, it will
> be beautiful. If it
> dies, then, too, it is
> good because one
> false relationship
> has ended.

your father, but you go on saying, "I am so glad to see you!" And
your whole being says, "Now leave me alone!" But verbally you go
on pretending. And they are doing the same thing; nobody becomes
aware because we are all moving in the same boat.

A religious person is one who comes out of this boat and risks his
life. He says, "Either I want to be true, or I don't want to be at all.
But I am not going to be false."

Whatsoever the stakes, try it, but don't go on moving in a false
way. The relationship may be strong enough. It may bear the truth.
Then it is very, very beautiful. If you cannot be true to the person
you love, then where will you be true? Where? If you cannot be true
to the person whom you think loves you—if you are afraid even with
them to reveal the truth, to be totally spiritually naked, if even there
you are hiding—then where will you find the place and space where
you can be totally free?

That's the meaning of love, that at least in one person's presence
we can be totally nude. We know that he loves, so he will not mis-

understand. We know that he loves, so the fear disappears. One can reveal all. One can open all the doors, one can invite the person to come in. One can start participating in another's being.

Love is participation, so at least with the lover don't be untrue. I'm not saying to go into the marketplace and be true because that will create unnecessary trouble right now. But start with the lover, then with the family, then with people who are farther away. By and by you will learn that to be true is so beautiful that you are willing to lose everything for it. Then in the marketplace—then truth simply becomes your way of life. The alphabet of love, truth, has to be learned with those who are very close because they will understand.

LEARN THE LANGUAGE OF SILENCE

You have always remained just casually related, and when you are formally related to someone, you can go on chattering about a thousand and one nonsensical things because nothing matters—it is just a pastime.

> When you start feeling closer to someone and an intimacy arises, then even a single word that you utter matters.

But when you start feeling closer to someone and an intimacy arises, then even a single word that you utter matters. Then you cannot play so easily with words because now everything is meaningful. So there will be gaps of silence. One feels awkward in the beginning because one is not accustomed to silence. One thinks something must be said, otherwise what will the other think?

Whenever you grow close, whenever there is some sort of love, silence comes, and there is nothing to say. In fact, there *is* nothing to say—there is nothing. With a stranger there is much to say; with friends, nothing to say. And the silence becomes heavy because you are not accustomed to it.

You don't know what the music of silence is. You know only one way of communicating, and that is verbal, through the mind. You don't know how to communicate through the heart, heart-to-heart, in silence. You don't know how to communicate by just being there, through your presence. You are growing, and the old pattern of communication is falling short. You will have to grow new patterns of communication, nonverbal. The more mature one becomes, the more nonverbal communication is needed.

Language is needed because we don't know how to communicate. When we know how to, by and by, language is not needed. Language is just a very primary-school medium. The real medium is of silence. So don't take a wrong attitude, otherwise you will stop growing. Nothing is missing when language starts to disappear; this is a wrong idea. Something new has come into being and the old pattern is not enough to contain it. You are growing, and your dresses are becoming short. It is not that something is missing; something is being added to you every day.

The more you meditate, the more you will love, and the more you will relate. And finally one comes to a moment when only silence helps. So next time when you are with somebody and you are not

> Language is needed because we don't know how to communicate. When we know how to, by and by, language is not needed.

communicating with words, and you are feeling very uneasy, feel happy. Become silent and allow that silence to communicate.

Language is needed to relate to people with whom you have no love relationship. Nonlanguage is needed for people with whom you have a love relationship. One has to become innocent again, like a child, and silent. Gestures will be there—sometimes you will smile and hold hands, or sometimes you will just remain silent, looking into each other's eyes, not doing anything, just being. The presences meet and merge, and something happens which only you will know. Only you to whom it has happened—no one else will become aware, it happens in such depth.

Enjoy that silence; feel and taste and savor it. Soon you will see that it has its own communication; that it is greater and higher and deeper and more profound. And that communication is sacred; it has a purity about it.

FOUR PITFALLS

People are afraid of great music, people are afraid of great poetry, people are afraid of deep intimacy. People's love affairs are just hit-and-run affairs. They don't go deep into each other's being because going deep into each other's being, the fear is there—the other's pool of being will reflect you. In that pool, in that mirror of the other's being, if you are not found—if the mirror remains empty, if it reflects nothing—then what?

THE HABIT OF REACTION

A reaction is out of the past; a response is out of the present. You react out of the past old patterns. Somebody insults you, suddenly the old mechanism starts functioning. In the past people have insulted you, and you have behaved in a certain way; you behave in the same way again. You are not responding to this insult and this person, you are simply repeating an old habit. You have not looked at this person and this new insult—it has a different flavor—you are just functioning like a robot. You have a certain mechanism inside you, you push the button, you say, "This man has insulted me," and you react. The reaction is not to the real situation, it is something projected. You have seen the past in this man.

It happened:

Buddha was sitting under a tree talking to his disciples. A man came and spit on his face. He wiped it off, and he asked the man, "What next? What do you want to say next?" The man was a little puzzled because he himself never expected that when you spit on somebody's face, he will ask, "What next?" He had had no such experience in his past. He had insulted people and they had become angry and they had reacted. Or if they were cowards and weaklings, they had smiled, trying to bribe the man. But Buddha was like neither; he was not angry nor in any way offended, nor in any way cowardly. But just matter-of-factly he said, "What next?" There was no reaction on his part.

Buddha's disciples became angry, they reacted. His closest disciple, Ananda, said, "This is too much, and we cannot tolerate it. You keep your teaching with you, and we will just show this man that he cannot do what he has done. He has to be punished for it. Otherwise everybody will start doing things like this."

Buddha said, "You keep silent. He has not offended me, but *you* are offending me. He is new, a stranger. He must have heard from people something about me, that 'this man is an atheist, a dangerous man who is throwing people off their track, a revolutionary, a corrupter.' And he may have formed some idea, a notion of me. He has not spit on me, he has spit on his notion, he has spit on his idea of me—because he does not know me at all, so how can he spit on me?

"If you think on it deeply," Buddha said, "he has spit on his own mind. I am not part of it, and I can see that this poor man must have something else to say because this is a way of saying something—spitting is a way of saying something. There are moments when you feel that language is impotent— in deep love, in intense anger, in hate, in prayer. There are intense moments when language is impotent. Then you have to do something. When you are in deep love and you kiss the person or embrace the person, what are you doing? You are saying something. When you are angry, intensely angry, you hit the person, you spit on him, you are saying something. I can understand him. He must have something more to say, that's why I'm asking, 'What next?' "

The man was even more puzzled! And Buddha said to his disciples, "I am more offended by you because you know me, and you have lived for years with me, and still you react."

Puzzled, confused, the man returned home. He could not sleep the whole night. When you see a buddha, it is difficult, impossible, to sleep again the way you used to sleep before. Again and again he was haunted by the experience. He could not explain it to himself, what had happened. He was trembling all over and perspiring. He had never come across such a man; he shattered his whole mind and his whole pattern, his whole past.

The next morning he was back there. He threw himself at Buddha's feet. Buddha asked him again, "What next? This, too, is a way of saying something that cannot be said in language. When you come and touch my feet, you are saying something that cannot be said ordinarily, for which all words are a little narrow; it cannot be contained in them." Buddha said, "Look, Ananda, this man is again here, he is saying some-thing. This man is a man of deep emotions."

The man looked at Buddha and said, "Forgive me for what I did yesterday."

Buddha said, "Forgive? <u>But I am not the same man</u> to whom you did it. The Ganges goes on flowing; it is never the same Ganges again. Every man is a river. The man you spit upon is no longer here—I look just like him, but I am not the same, much has happened in these twenty-four hours! The river has flowed so much. So I cannot forgive you be-cause I have no grudge against you.

"And you also are new. I can see you are not the same man who came yesterday because that man was angry—he was anger! He spit, whereas you are bowing at my feet, touch-ing my feet—how can you be the same man? You are not the same man, so let us forget about it. Those two people—the man who spit, and the man on whom he spit—both are no more. Come closer. Let us talk of something else."

This is response.

Reaction is out of the past. If you react out of old habits, out of mind, then you are not responding. <u>To be responsive is to be totally alive in this moment, here now.</u> Response is a beautiful phenome-non, it is life. <u>Reaction is dead, ugly</u>, rot-ten; it is a corpse. Ninety-nine per cent of the time you react and you call it re-sponse. Rarely it happens in your life

> If you react out of old habits, out of mind, then you are not responding. To be responsive is to be totally alive in this moment, here now.

that you respond; but whenever it happens, you have a glimpse. Whenever it happens, the door to the unknown opens.

Go back to your home and look at your wife with response, not with reaction. I see people, they may have lived with a woman for thirty years, forty years, and they have stopped looking at her! They know she is the "old lady," the old woman they think they know. But the river has been flowing all the time. This woman is not the same one to whom they got married. That is a past phenomenon, that woman exists nowhere now; this is totally a new woman.

Every moment you are being born anew. Every moment you die, and every moment you are born. But have you looked lately at your wife, your mother, your father, your friend? You have stopped looking because you think they are all old, and what is the point of looking at them. Go back and look again with fresh eyes, as you would look at a stranger, and you will be surprised at how much this old woman has changed.

Tremendous changes happen every day. It is a flux. Everything goes on flowing, nothing is frozen. But the mind is a dead thing, it is a frozen phenomenon. If you act from the frozen mind, you live a dead life. You don't live really—you are already in the grave.

> Have you looked lately at your wife, your mother, your father, your friend? Go back and look again with fresh eyes, as you would look at a stranger, and you will be surprised.

Drop reactions. And allow more and more responses. To be responsive is to be responsible. To be responsive, to be responding, is to be sensitive. But sensitive to here and now.

STUCK ON SECURITY

No relationship can be secure. It is not the nature of relationships to be secure, and if any relationship is secure, it will lose all attraction. So this is a problem for the mind. If you want to enjoy a relationship, it has to be insecure. If you make it completely secure, absolutely secure, then you cannot enjoy it—it loses all charm, all attraction. The mind cannot be satisfied either with this or with that, so it is always in conflict and chaos. It wants a relationship that is alive and secure, but this is impossible because an alive person, or an alive relationship, or anything that is alive, has to be unpredictable. What is going to happen in the next moment cannot be forecast. And because it is unpredictable, this moment becomes intense.

> An alive person, or an alive relationship, or anything that is alive, has to be unpredictable. What is going to happen in the next moment cannot be forecast.

You have to live this moment as totally as possible because the next moment may not come ever. You may not be there; the other may not be there. Or you may both be there, but the relationship is not. All possibilities remain open. The future always remains open, the past is always closed. And in between the two is the present, a single moment of present, always trembling, shaking. But this is how life is. The shaking and the trembling are part of being alive—the hesitation, the cloudiness, the vagueness.

The past is closed. Everything has happened, and now nothing can be changed, so everything is absolutely closed. The future is absolutely open, nothing can be predicted. And between the two is the present, with one foot in the past, one in the future. So the mind always remains in a dichotomy, in a divided state. It is always split, it is always schizophrenic.

You need to understand that this is how things are, and nothing can be done about it. If you want to have a very secure relationship, then you will have to love a dead man; but then you will not enjoy it. That's what happens to a lover when he becomes a husband—a husband is a dead lover, a wife is a dead lover. The past has become all, and now the past decides the future. In fact, if you are a wife you don't have a future—the past will go on repeating itself, all the doors are closed. If you are a husband, then you don't have a future; then you are confined, in an imprisonment.

So security is sought continuously, but when you find it you get fed up with it. Look at the faces of husbands and wives. They have found security—the much-sought-after security—and now everything is in their bank balance, and the law and the court and the constable are all there to make everything secure. But now the whole charm, the whole poetry, is lost; romance is no more. Now they are dead people—they are simply repeating the past, they live in memories.

Listen to wives and husbands talking. The wife goes on saying that the husband doesn't love her as he used to, and they go on talking about past moments, their honeymoon and other

> Look at the faces of husbands and wives. They have found security—the much-sought-after security—and now everything is in their bank balance. But now the whole charm, the whole poetry, is lost, romance is no more.

things. What nonsense! You are still alive. This moment can be a honeymoon. This moment can be lived, but you are talking of the past and trying to repeat it.

> If you want to love a person, love them here, now. Love them. Because nobody knows what is going to happen in the next moment.

Security never satisfies—and in insecurity there is fear, fear that the relationship can be lost. But that is part of being alive. Everything can be lost, nothing is certain, and that's why everything is so beautiful. And that's why you need not postpone for a single moment—if you want to love a person, love them here, now. Love them. Because nobody knows what is going to happen in the next moment. The next moment there may be no possibility for love, and then you will repent for the whole of your life. You could have loved, you could have lived. Then remorse surrounds a person, repentance and a deep guilt is felt, as if you have been committing suicide.

Life is uncertain. No one can make it certain. There is no way to make it certain. And it is good that nobody can make it certain; otherwise, it would be dead. Life is fragile, delicate, always moving into the unknown; that's its beauty. One needs to be courageous, adventurous. One needs to be a gambler to move with life. So be a gambler. Live this moment, and live it totally. When the next moment comes, we will see. You will be there to tackle it—as you have been able to tackle the past, you will be able to tackle the future also—and you will be more capable because you will be more experienced.

So it is not a question of whether the other is going to be there the next moment. The question is that if he is available to you in this moment, love him. Don't waste this moment in thinking and worrying about the future because this is suicidal. Don't pay a single thought to the future because nothing can be done about it, so it is a sheer waste of energy. Love this man and be loved by him.

This is my understanding: that if you live this moment totally, there is every possibility that in the next moment the person may be still available. I say *may be*—I can't promise you. But the possibility is greater because the next moment is going to come out of this one. If you have loved the man, and the man feels blessed, and the relationship has been a beautiful experience, an ecstasy, then why should he leave you?

In fact, if you go on worrying, you are making him, forcing him, to leave you. And if you have wasted this moment, the next moment will come out of this wastage; it is going to be rotten. And that is how one becomes self-predictable. You go on fulfilling your own prophecies. The next moment you say, "Yes, I was saying from the very beginning that this relationship was not going to last. Now it is proven." Then you feel very good in a way; you feel you have been very clever and wise. In fact, you have been foolish because it is not that you predicted anything. You forced this event to happen because you wasted the time, the opportunity, that was given to you. So love the person and forget about the future. Just drop the whole nonsense of thinking about it. If you can love, love.

> If you live this moment totally, there is every possibility that in the next moment the person may be still available. I say *may be*—I can't promise you. But the possibility is greater because the next moment is going to come out of this one.

> You go on fulfilling your own prophecies. The next moment you say, "Yes, I was saying from the very beginning that this relationship was not going to last. Now it is proven." Then you feel very good in a way, you feel you have been very clever and wise.

If you cannot love, forget this one, find somebody else. But don't waste time.

The question is not of this lover or that lover, the question is of love. Love fulfills, people are just excuses. But the whole thing depends on you because whatsoever you are doing with one person, you will go on doing with another.

If you make a person happy, why should he leave you? But if you make him unhappy, then why shouldn't he leave you? If you make him unhappy, then I will help him to leave you! But if you make him happy, nobody can help him to leave you; then there is no point; he will fight the whole world for you.

So become happier. Use the time that you have—and there is no need to think about the future; the present is enough. From this very moment, try to live this moment. Use this moment not in worrying but in living. Small things can become so beautiful. A little caring, a little sharing, that's all life is.

EVERY MAN CREATES A CERTAIN PSYCHOLOGICAL SECURITY, unaware of the fact that his security is his prison. People are surrounded by all kinds of insecurities; hence the natural desire is to create a protection. This protection becomes bigger and bigger as you become more alert to the dangers you are living through. Your prison cell becomes smaller; you start living so well protected that life itself becomes impossible.

Life is possible only in insecurity. This is something very fundamental to be understood: Life in its very essence is insecurity. While you are protecting yourself, you are destroying your very life. Protection is death because only those who are dead in their graves are absolutely protected. Nobody can harm them, nothing can go wrong for them.

> If you make a person happy, why should he leave you? But if you make him unhappy, then why shouldn't he leave you?

There is no longer any death for them, all that has happened. Nothing more is going to happen.

Do you want the security of a graveyard? Unknowingly that's what everybody is trying to do. Their ways are different, but the goal is the same. By money, by power, by prestige, by social conformity, by belonging to a herd—religious, political—by being part of a family, a nation, what are you seeking? An unknown fear surrounds you, and you start creating as many barriers as possible between you and the fear. But those same barriers are going to prevent you from living. Once this is understood, you will know the meaning of *sannyas*. It is accepting life as insecurity, dropping all defenses and allowing life to take possession of you. This is a dangerous step, but those who are capable of taking it are rewarded immensely because only they live. Others just survive.

There is a difference between survival and living. Survival is only a dragging—dragging from the cradle to the grave, wondering when the grave is going to come. In the space between the cradle and the

> Only those who are dead in their graves are absolutely protected. Nobody can harm them, nothing can go wrong for them.

grave, why be afraid? Death is certain . . . and you don't have anything to lose. You come without anything. Your fears are just projections. You don't have anything to lose, and one day what you have is bound to disappear. If death were uncertain, there would be some substance in the idea of creating security. If you could avoid death, then naturally it would be perfectly right to create barriers between you and death. But you cannot avoid it. Death is there—once accepted it loses all power, nothing can be done about it. When nothing can be done about it, then why be bothered?

It is a well-known fact that soldiers going to the war are trembling. Deep down they know that all will not be returning back in the evening. Who will return and who will not return is not known, but it is possible that perhaps they themselves may not be returning home. But psychologists have been observing a strange phenomenon: As the soldiers reach the war front, all their fears disappear. They start fighting very playfully. Once death is accepted, then where is its sting? Once they know that death is possible at any moment, then they can forget all about it. I have been with many army people, I had many friends in the army, and it was strange to see that they are the most joyous people, the most relaxed. Any day the call can come—"join the forces"—but they play cards, they play golf, they drink, they dance. They enjoy life to the fullest.

One of the generals used to come to me. I asked him, "You are prepared almost every day for death—how can you manage still to be happy?"

He said, "What else is there to do? Death is certain."

Once the certainty, unavoidability, inescapability is accepted, then rather than crying and weeping and complaining and dragging yourself toward the grave, why not dance? Why not make the most of the time that you have between the cradle and the grave? Why not live every moment to such totality that if the next moment never comes, there is no complaint? You can die joyously because you have lived joyously.

But very few people have understood the inner working of their own psychology. Rather than living, they start protecting. The same energy that could have become a song and a dance becomes involved in creating more money, more power, more ambition, more security. The same energy that could have been a tremendously beautiful flower of love becomes just an imprisonment in a marriage.

> Rather than crying and weeping and complaining and dragging yourself toward the grave, why not dance? Why not live every moment to such totality that if the next moment never comes, there is no complaint?

Marriage is secure—by law, by social convention, by your own idea of respectability and what people will say. Everybody is afraid of everybody else, so people go on pretending. Love disappears—it is not in your hands. It comes just like the breeze comes, and it goes just like the breeze goes. Those who are alert and aware dance with the breeze, relish it to its deepest potential, enjoy its coolness and fragrance. And when it is gone, they are not sorry and sad. It was a gift from the unknown. It may come again. They wait—and it comes again and again. They learn, slowly, a deep patience and waiting. But most human beings down the centuries have done the very opposite. Afraid that the breeze may escape, they close all the doors, all the windows, all possible cracks from where it can escape. This is their arrangement for security; this is called marriage. But now they are shocked—when all the windows and the doors are closed, and they have plugged even small cracks, instead of having a great, cool, fragrant breeze they have only a stale, dead air! Everybody feels it, but it needs courage to recognize that they have destroyed the beauty of the breeze by capturing it.

In life, nothing can be captured and imprisoned. One has to live in openness, allowing all kinds of experiences to happen, being fully grateful as long as they last. Thankful, but not afraid of tomorrow. If today has brought a beautiful morning, a beautiful sunrise, songs of birds, great flowers, why be worried about tomorrow? Because tomorrow will be another today. Maybe the sunrise will have different colors. Maybe the birds will change their songs a little, maybe there will be rain clouds and the dance of the rain. But that has its own beauty, that has its own nourishment.

It is good that things go on changing; that every evening is not the same, that every day is not exactly a repetition. Something new—that is the very excitement and ecstasy of life, otherwise man will be so bored. And those who have made their life completely secure are bored. They are bored with their wives, they are bored with their children, they

> In life, nothing can be captured and imprisoned. One has to live in openness, allowing all kinds of experiences to happen, being fully grateful as long as they last.

are bored with their friends. Boredom is the experience of millions of people, although they smile to hide it.

Friedrich Nietzsche says, "Don't think I am a happy man. I smile just to prevent my tears. I become busy in smiling so I can prevent my tears. If I don't smile, tears are bound to come." Completely wrong attitudes have been taught to people: Hide your tears, remain always at a distance, keep others at least at arm's length. Don't allow others too close because then they may know your inner misery, your boredom, your anguish; they may know your sickness.

The whole of humanity is sick for the simple reason that we have not allowed life's insecurity to be our very religion. Our gods are our security, our virtues are our security, our knowledge is our security, our relationships are our securities. We are wasting our whole lives in accumulating security bonds. Our virtues, austerities, are nothing but an effort to be secure even after death. It is creating a bank balance in the other world.

But meanwhile a tremendously beautiful life is slipping out of your hands. The trees are so beautiful because they don't know the fear of insecurity. The wild animals have such grandeur because they don't know that there is death, that there is insecurity. The flowers can dance in the sun and in the rain because they are not concerned about what is going to happen in the evening. Their petals will fall, and just as they had appeared from an unknown source they will disappear back into the same unknown source. But meanwhile, between these two points of appearance and disappearance, you have the opportunity either to dance or to despair.

An authentic person simply drops the idea of security and starts living in utter insecurity because that is the nature of life. You cannot change it. That which you cannot change, accept—and accept it with joy. Don't unnecessarily hit your head against the wall, just pass through the door.

SHADOWBOXING

A parable from Chuang Tzu:

> *There was a man who was so disturbed by the sight of his own shadow and so displeased with his own footsteps that he determined to get rid of both.*
>
> *The method he hit upon was to run away from them, so he got up and ran, but every time he put his foot down, there was another step, while his shadow kept up with him without the slightest difficulty.*
>
> *He attributed his failure to the fact that he was not running fast enough. So he ran faster and faster, without stopping, until he finally dropped dead.*
>
> *He failed to realize that if he merely stepped into the shade, his shadow would vanish, and if he sat down and stayed still, there would be no more footsteps.*

Man creates his own confusion just because he goes on rejecting himself, condemning himself, not accepting himself. Then a chain of confusion, inner chaos, and misery is created. Why don't you accept yourself as you are? What is wrong? The whole of existence accepts you as you are, but you don't.

You have some ideal to achieve. That ideal is always in the future—it has to be; no ideal can be in the present. And the future is nowhere; it is not yet born. But because of the ideal, you live in the future—which is nothing but a dream. Because of the ideal, you cannot live here and now. Because of the ideal, you condemn yourself.

All ideologies, all ideals, are condemnatory because they create an image in the mind. And when you go on comparing yourself with that image, you will always feel that something is lacking, something is missing. Nothing is lacking, and nothing is missing. You are perfect as far as there is any possibility of perfection.

Try to understand this because only then will you be able to understand Chuang Tzu's parable. It is one of the most beautiful parables that anybody has ever talked about, and it goes very deep into the very mechanism of the human mind. Why do you go on carrying ideals in the mind? Why are you not enough as you are? Just at this moment why are you not like gods? Who is interfering? Who is blocking your path? This very moment why can't you enjoy and be blissful? Where is the block?

The block comes through the ideal. How can you enjoy? You are filled with so much anger, first the anger has to go. How can you be blissful? You are filled with so much sexuality, first the sex has to go. How can you be like gods celebrating this very moment? You are filled with so much greed, passion, anger, first they have to go. Then you will be like gods.

This is how the ideal is created, and because of the ideal you

> All ideologies, all ideals, are condemnatory because they create an image in the mind. And when you go on comparing yourself with that image, you will always feel that something is lacking.

become condemned. Compare yourself with the ideal, and you will never be perfect. It is impossible. If you say, "if," then bliss is impossible because that "if" is the greatest disturbance.

If you say, "If those conditions are fulfilled, then I will be blissful," then these conditions are never going to be fulfilled. And secondly, even if these conditions are fulfilled, by that time you will have lost the very capacity to celebrate and enjoy. And moreover, when these conditions are fulfilled—if ever, because they cannot be fulfilled—your mind will create further ideals.

This is how you have been missing life for lives together. You create an ideal, and then you want to be that ideal; then you feel condemned and inferior. Because of your dreaming mind, your reality is condemned; dreams have been disturbing you.

I tell you just the opposite. Be like gods this very moment. Let there be anger, let there be sex, let there be greed—you celebrate life. And by and by you will feel more celebration, less anger; more blissfulness, less greed; more joy, less sex. Then you have hit upon the right path. It is not otherwise. When a person can celebrate life in its totality, all that is wrong disappears. But if you try first to make arrangements for the wrong to disappear, it never disappears.

It is just like fighting with darkness. Your house is filled with darkness and you ask, "How can I light a candle? Before I light a candle this darkness has to be dispelled." This is what you have been doing. You say that first greed must go; then there will be ecstasy. You are foolish! You are saying that first the darkness must go, and then you can light a candle, as if darkness can hinder you. Darkness is a nonentity. It is nothing, it has no solidity. It is just an absence, not a presence. It is just the absence of light—light the light, and darkness disappears.

Celebrate, become a blissful flame, and all that is wrong disappears.

Anger, greed, sex, or whatsoever else you name are not solid; they are just the absence of a blissful, ecstatic life.

Because you cannot enjoy, you are angry. It is not that somebody creates your anger; because you cannot enjoy, you are in much misery. That is why you are angry. Others are only excuses. Because you cannot celebrate, love cannot happen to you—hence sex. That is settling for shadows. And then the mind says, "First destroy these, and then God will descend." It is one of the most patent stupidities of humanity, the most ancient, and it follows everybody.

It is difficult for you to think that at this very moment you are gods, but I ask you, what is lacking? What is missing? You are alive, breathing, conscious, what else do you need? This very moment be like gods. Even if you feel that it is just an "as if," don't bother. Even if you feel, "I am just presuming that I am like a god," presume—don't bother. Start with the "as if," and soon the reality will follow because in reality you *are*. And once you start existing as a god, all misery, all confusion, all darkness disappears. Become a light, and this becoming has no conditions to be fulfilled.

Now I will enter this beautiful parable:

There was a man who was so disturbed by the sight of his own shadow and so displeased with his own footsteps that he determined to get rid of both.

Remember, you are this man—this man exists in everybody. This is how you have been behaving, this is also your logic: flight from the shadow. This man was much disturbed by the sight of his own shadow. Why? What is wrong with a shadow? Why should you be disturbed by a shadow? Because, you may have heard, dreamers have said that gods have no shadows. When they walk, no shadow is created. This man was disturbed because of these gods.

It is said that in heaven the sun rises and gods walk, but they don't have any shadows, they are transparent. But I tell you: This is just a dream. Nowhere does anything exist, can anything exist, without a shadow. If it *is,* then a shadow will be created. If it is *not,* only then can the shadow disappear.

To be means to create a shadow. Your anger, your sex, your greed—all are shadows. But remember they are shadows. They are in a sense, and still they are not, that is the meaning of a shadow. It is nonsubstantial. A shadow is just an absence. You stand, the sun's rays fall on you, and because of you, a few rays cannot pass. Then the figure is created, the figure of the shadow. It is just an absence. You obstruct the sun; that is why the shadow is created.

The shadow is not substantial, *you* are substantial. You are substantial; that is why the shadow is created. If you were like a ghost, then there would be no shadow. And the angels in heaven are nothing but ghosts, ghosts dreamed up by you and your ideologists, men who create ideals. This man was disturbed because he had heard that you become a god only when the shadow disappears.

> 🖉
>
> What are your disturbances? If you go deep, you will find nothing but the sound of your footsteps.

There was a man who was so disturbed by the sight of his own shadow and so displeased with his own footsteps that he determined to get rid of both.

What are your disturbances? If you go deep, you will find nothing but the sound of your footsteps. Why are you so disturbed by the sound of your footsteps? You are substantial, so there must be a little sound; one has to accept this. But the man had heard the story that gods have no shadows, and when they walk no sound of footsteps is created. These gods can be nothing but dream objects; they exist only in the mind. This heaven exists nowhere! Whenever something exists, sound is created around it. This is how things are, you cannot do anything about it. This is how nature is. If you try to do something about it, you will go wrong. If you try to do something about it, your whole life will be wasted, and in the end you will feel that you have not reached anywhere. The shadow remains, the footsteps make sounds, and death is knocking at the door.

Before death knocks, accept yourself, and then a miracle happens. That miracle is that when you accept yourself, you don't run away from yourself. Right now, each one of you is running away from himself. Even if you come to me, you come to me as part of your escape from yourself. That is why you cannot reach me; that is the gap. If you have come to me as an escape from yourself you cannot come to me because my whole effort is to help you not to escape from yourself. Don't try to escape from yourself; you cannot be anybody else. You have a definite destiny and individuality.

Just as your thumb makes a print, unique and individual—that type of thumb has never existed before and will never exist again, it belongs only to you, there will never be another like it—the same is the case with your being. You have a being unique and individual, incomparable; it has never been before, it

> You have a being unique and individual, incomparable, it has never been before, it will never be again, only you have it. Celebrate it!

will never be again, only you have it. Celebrate it! Something unique has happened to everyone, God has given a unique gift to everyone, and you condemn it. You want something better! You try to be wiser than the existence, you try to be wiser than Tao, then you go wrong.

Remember, the part can never be wiser than the whole, and whatsoever the whole is doing is the final thing, you cannot change. You can make an effort to do so and waste your life, but nothing will be achieved through it.

> Why not say yes to the shadow? The moment you say yes, you forget it; it disappears—from the mind at least, even if it remains with the body.

The whole is vast; you are just an atomic cell. The ocean is vast, you are just a drop in it. The whole ocean is salty, and you are trying to be sweet—it is impossible. But the ego wants to do the impossible, the difficult, that which cannot be done. And Chuang Tzu says, "Easy is right." Why can't you be easy and accepting? Why not say yes to the shadow? The moment you say yes, you forget it; it disappears—from the mind at least, even if it remains with the body.

But what is the problem? How does a shadow create a problem? Why make a problem out of it? As you are right now, you make a problem out of everything. This man was puzzled, disturbed, by the sight of his own shadow. He would have liked to be a god, he would have liked to be shadowless.

But you are already like a god, and you cannot be anything that you are not already. How can you be? You can only be that which you are—all becoming is just moving toward the being, which is already there. You may wander and knock on others' doors, but this is just playing hide and seek with yourself. It is up to you how much you knock on others' doors and how much you wander here and there. Finally you will come to your own door, and to the realization that your own door has always been there. Nobody can take it away. Nature, the Tao, cannot be taken away from you.

This man was disturbed because of his shadow. The method he hit upon was to run away from it—that is the method everybody hits upon. It seems that the mind has a vicious logic. For example, if you feel angry, what will you do? The mind will say, "Don't be angry, take a vow." What will you do? You will suppress it—and the more you suppress, the more the anger will move to the very roots of your being. Then you will not be sometimes angry and sometimes not angry; if you have suppressed too much, you will be *continuously* angry. It will become your blood, it will be a poison all over; it will spread into all your relationships. Even if you are in love with someone, the anger will be there and the love will become violent. Even if you try to help somebody, in that help there will be poison because the poison is in you. And all your acts will carry it, they will reflect you. When you feel this again, the mind will say, "You have not been suppressing enough, suppress more." Anger is there because of suppression, and the mind says, "Suppress it more!" Then there will be more anger.

Your mind is sexual because of suppression, and the mind says, "Suppress it more. Find new methods and ways and means to suppress it more so that celibacy will flower." But it cannot flower that way. Through suppression, sex not only goes into the body, it goes into the mind, it becomes cerebral. Then a person goes on thinking about it, again and again. Hence so much pornographic literature in the world.

Why do people like to see pictures of naked women? Are women themselves not enough? They are, they are more than enough! So what is the need? The picture is always more sexual than a real woman. A real woman has a body and a shadow, and her footsteps will be there, and sound will be created. A photograph is a dream; it is absolutely mental, cerebral, and it has no shadow. A real woman will perspire and there will be a smell of the body; a picture never perspires. A real woman will be angry; a picture is never angry. A real woman will age, will become old; a picture always remains young and fresh. A picture is just mental. Those who suppress sex in the body become mentally sexual. Then their mind moves in sexuality, and then it is a disease.

If you feel hungry it is okay, eat; but if you think about food continuously, then it is an obsession and a disease. When you feel hungry it is okay if you eat and are finished with it. But you are never finished with anything, and everything goes into the mind.

Mulla Nasruddin's wife was ill and she had been operated on. A few days earlier she had come back home from the hospital, so I asked, "How is your wife? Has she recovered from the operation?" He said, "No, she is still talking about it."

If you are thinking about something, talking about something, it is there. And now it is more dangerous because the body will recover, but the mind can go on and on and on, ad infinitum. The body may recover, but the mind will never recover.

If you suppress hunger in the body, it goes into the mind. The problem has not been thrown out, it has been pushed in. Suppress anything and it goes to the roots. Then the mind will say that if you are not succeeding, something is wrong, you are not making enough effort; make more effort.

The method he hit upon was to run away from them.

Mind has only two alternatives, fight or flight. Whenever there is a problem, the mind says either fight it or escape from it—and both are wrong. If you fight, you remain with the problem. If you fight, the problem will be there continuously. If you fight, you are divided because the problem is not outside, the problem is inside.

For example, if there is anger and you fight, what will happen? Half of your being will be with the anger and half with this idea of fight. It is as if both your hands are fighting each other. Who is going to win? You will be simply dissipating energy. No one is going to be victorious. You can fool yourself that you now have your anger suppressed, you are now sitting on your anger. But then you will have to sit on it continuously—not even a single moment's holiday is allowed. If you forget about it for a single moment, you will lose your whole victory.

So people who have suppressed something are always sitting on those suppressed things, and they are always afraid. They cannot relax. Why has relaxation become so difficult? Why can't you sleep? Why can't you relax? Why can't you be in a let-go? Because you have suppressed so many things. You are afraid that if you relax, they will come up. Your so-called religious people cannot relax; they are tense, and the tension is because of this. They have suppressed something—and you say to relax? They know that if they relax, the enemy will come up. The mind thinks, either fight—and if you fight, then you suppress—or escape. But where will you escape to? Even if you go to the Himalayas, the an-

> Why can't you relax? Because you have suppressed so many things. You are afraid that if you relax, they will come up.

83

ger will follow you; it is your shadow. The sex will follow you; it is your shadow. Wherever you go, your shadow will be with you.

The method he hit upon was to run away from them. So he got up and ran, but every time he put his foot down there was another step, while his shadow kept up with him without the slightest difficulty.

He was surprised! He was running so fast, but there was no difficulty for the shadow. The shadow was following easily, not even perspiring, not breathing hard. There was no difficulty on the part of the shadow because a shadow is not substantial, a shadow is nobody. The man may have been perspiring, he may have had difficulty breathing but the shadow was always in step with him. The shadow cannot leave you in this way. Neither fight nor flight will help. Where will you go? Wherever you go, you will carry yourself with you, and your shadow will be there.

> One has to understand the logic of the mind. If you don't understand, you will be a victim of it.

He attributed his failure to the fact that he was not running fast enough. So he ran faster and faster, without stopping, until he finally dropped dead.

One has to understand the logic of the mind. If you don't understand, you will be a victim of it. The mind has a vicious logic, it is a vicious circle, it is circular. If you listen to it, then every step will lead you more and more in the circle. This man is perfectly logical; you cannot find any fault, any flaw, in his logic. There is no loophole; he is as perfect a logician as any Aristotle. He says that if the shadow is following him, it shows that he is not running fast enough. He must run faster and faster; then the moment will come when the shadow will not be able to follow him. But the shadow is yours, it is not somebody else following you. If it were, then the logic would have been right.

If somebody else had been following this man, then he would have been right, absolutely right: He was not running fast enough, and that was why the other was following. But he was wrong because there was nobody else. The mind was useless.

Mind for others, meditation for yourself. Mind for others, no-mind for yourself—that is the whole emphasis of Chuang Tzu or Zen or the Sufis or Hasids, of all those who know; of Buddha, Jesus, Muhammad, of all those who have known. The whole emphasis is that you can use the mind for others, no-mind for yourself.

This man got into trouble because he used the mind for himself, and the mind has its own pattern. The mind said, "Faster, faster! If you go fast enough, this shadow will not be able to follow you."

He attributed his failure to the fact that he was not running fast enough.

The failure was there in the first place because he was running. But the mind cannot say that, the mind has not been fed for it. It is a computer, you have to feed it; it is a mechanism. It cannot give you anything new; it can only give you whatsoever you have fed into it. The mind cannot give you anything new; whatsoever it gives you is borrowed. And if you are addicted to listening to it, always you will be in trouble when you turn toward yourself. When there is a conversion, a turning toward the source, then you will be in difficulty.

Then this mind is absolutely useless—not only useless, it is a positive hindrance, it is harmful. So drop it.

I have heard:

It happened that one day Mulla Nasruddin's son came home from his progressive school and brought a book on sexology. His mother was very much disturbed, but she waited for Mulla Nasruddin to come. Something had to be done; this progressive school was going too far! When Mulla Nasruddin came, his wife showed him the book.

Nasruddin went upstairs to find his son. He found him in his room, kissing the maidservant. So Nasruddin said, "Son, when you are finished with your homework, come down."

This is logical! Logic has its own steps, and each step follows another, there is no end to it. The man frightened by his shadow followed the mind, so he ran faster and faster without stopping until he finally dropped dead. Faster and faster without stopping . . . then only death can occur.

Have you ever observed that life has not occurred to you yet? Have you observed that there has never been a single moment of *life as such* happening to you? You have not experienced a single moment of the bliss that Chuang Tzu and Buddha talk about. And what is going to happen to you? Nothing is going to happen to you except death. And the nearer you come to death, the faster you run because you think that if you go faster, you will escape.

Where are you going so fast? Man and man's mind have always been mad about speed, as if we are going somewhere and speed is needed. So we go on becoming more and more speedy. Where are you going? Finally, whether you go slow or fast, you reach death. And everybody arrives at the right moment, not a single moment is lost. Everybody reaches there right on time, nobody is ever late. I have heard that a few people have reached death before their time, but I have never heard of anybody reaching death late. Some people reach the end before their time because of their doctors. . . .

He attributed his failure to the fact that he was not running fast enough. So he ran faster and faster, without stopping, until he finally dropped dead. He failed to realize that if he merely stepped into the shade, his shadow would vanish.

Easy it was, the easiest! If you just move into the shade where the sun is not, the shadow disappears because a shadow is created by the sun. It is the absence of the sun's rays. If you are under a tree in the shade, the shadow disappears.

He failed to realize that if he merely stepped into the shade, his shadow would vanish.

That shade is called silence, that shade is called inner peace. Don't listen to the mind. Just step into the shade, into the inner silence where no rays of the sun enter.

You remain on the periphery, that is the problem. There you are in the light of the outside world, and shadow is created. Close your eyes, move into the shade. The moment you close your eyes, the sun is no longer there. Hence all meditations are done with closed eyes— you are moving into your own shade. Inside there is no sun and no shadow. Outside is society, and outside are all types of shadows. Have you ever realized that your anger, your sex, your greed, your ambition, are all part of society? If you really move in and leave society out,

87

where is anger? Where is sex? But remember, in the beginning when you close your eyes they are not really closed. You carry images from the outside inside, and you will find the same society reflected. But if you continue simply moving, moving, moving inside, sooner or later society will be left out. You are in, society is out—you have moved from the periphery to the center.

In this center there is a silence: no anger and no antianger, no sex and no celibacy, no greed and no nongreed, no violence, no nonviolence—because those are all outside. Remember, the opposites are also outside—inside you are neither this nor that. You are simply a being, pure. This is what I mean, being like a god—a pure being with no opposites hanging around, fighting or flighting. No, simply being. You have moved into the shade.

> The mind always finds it easier to run, to fight, because then there is something to do. If you say to the mind, "Don't do anything," that is the most difficult thing.

He failed to realize that if he only moved into the shade then his shadow would vanish.

And if he sat down and stayed still, there could be no more footsteps. It was really so easy. But that which is easy is so difficult for the mind because the mind always finds it easier to run, to fight, because then there is something to do. If you say to the mind, "Don't do anything," that is the most difficult thing. The mind will ask, "Give me a mantra at least, so that with closed eyes I can say Aum, Aum . . . Ram, Ram. Something to do because how can we remain without doing anything,

> Mind is activity, and being is absolute inactivity. Mind is running, being is sitting. The periphery is moving, the center is not moving.

without something to run after, to chase?"

Mind is activity, and being is absolute inactivity. Mind is running, being is sitting. The periphery is moving, the center is not moving. Look at a wagon wheel moving—the wheel is moving but the center around which the whole wheel moves is static, absolutely static, nonmoving. Your being is eternally unmoving, and your periphery is continuously moving. This is the point to remember in Sufi Dervish dancing, the whirling meditation. When you do it, let the body become the periphery—the body moves, and you are eternally unmoving. Become a wheel. The body becomes the wheel, the periphery, and you are the center. Soon you will realize that although the body goes on moving faster and faster and faster, inside you can feel that you are not moving; and the faster the body moves, the better because then the contrast is created. Suddenly the body and you are separate.

But you move with the body continuously, so there is no separation. Go and sit. Simply sitting is enough, not doing anything. Simply close your eyes and sit and sit and sit, and allow everything to settle. It will take time because you have been unsettled for so many lives. You have been trying to create all sorts of disturbances. It will take time—but only time. You need not do anything; you simply look and sit, look and sit. . . . Zen people call it *Zazen*. Zazen means just sitting, not doing anything.

This is what Chuang Tzu says:

He failed to realize that if he merely stepped into the shade, his shadow would vanish, and if he sat down and stayed still, there would be no more footsteps.

There was no need to fight, and there was no need to escape. The only thing needed was just to move into the shade and sit still.

And this is to be done during your whole life. Don't fight with anything, and don't try to escape from anything. Let things take their own course. You simply close your eyes and move inside to the center where no sun's ray has ever penetrated. There is no shadow—and really, that is the meaning of the myth that gods have no shadows. Not that there are gods somewhere who have no shadows, but the god that is within you has no shadow because no outside penetrates there. It cannot penetrate; it is always in the shade.

Chuang Tzu calls that shade *Tao,* your innermost nature—utterly innermost, absolutely innermost.

So what is to be done? One, don't listen to the mind. It is a good tool for the outside, but it is absolutely a barrier for the inside. Logic is good for other people; it is not good for yourself. In tackling *things,* logic and doubt are needed. Science depends on doubt, and religiousness depends on faith, trust. Just sit, with a deep trust that your inner nature will take over. It always takes over. You have only to wait, only patience is needed. And whatsoever your mind says, simply don't listen to it.

Listen to the mind for the outside world; don't listen to the mind for the inside—simply put it aside. And there is no need to fight with it because if you fight with it, it may influence you. You simply put it aside. That's what faith is. Faith is not a fight with the mind—if you fight, then the enemy impresses you. And remember, even friends don't have such an impact as enemies have. If you fight with someone continuously, you will be influenced by them because you will have to use the same techniques to fight them. Ultimately, enemies become similar. It is very difficult to be aloof and detached from the enemy; the enemy influences you.

And those who start fighting with the mind become great philosophers. They may talk about antimind, but their whole talk is of the mind. They may say, "Be against the mind," but whatsoever they say is coming from the mind, even their enmity. You have to remain with your enemy, and by and by enemies settle terms, and they become the same.

Always remember: Don't fight with the mind. Otherwise you will have to yield to the terms. If you want to convince the mind, you have to be argu-

> Even friends don't have such an impact as enemies have. If you fight with someone continuously, you will be influenced by them because you will have to use the same techniques to fight them.

mentative, and that is the whole point. If you have to convince the mind, you have to use words, and that is the whole problem. Simply put it aside. This putting aside is not against mind, it is beyond mind. It is simply putting it aside. Just as when you go out you use your shoes, and when you come in you put them aside—there is no fight, nothing. You don't say to the shoes, "Now I am going in, and you are not needed, so I will put you aside." You simply put them aside; they are not needed.

Just like this—easy is right—there is no fight. Easy is right—there is no struggle and conflict. You simply put the mind aside, move into the inner shade, and sit. Then no footsteps are heard, and no shadow follows you. You become godlike. And you can become only that

which you are already. So I tell you, you are godlike, you are gods.
Don't settle for less than that.

FALSE VALUES

One very fundamental thing has to be remembered: Man is very clever
in creating false values. The real values demand your totality, demand
your whole being; the false values are very cheap. They look like the
real, but they don't demand your totality—just a superficial formality.

For example, in place of love, trust, we have created a false value,
"loyalty." The loyal person is only superficially concerned with love.
He goes through all the gestures of love, but he means nothing by
them; his heart stays out of his formal gestures.

A slave is loyal—but do you think anybody who is a slave, who
has been reduced in his humanity, whose whole pride and dignity have
been taken away, can love the person who has harmed him so deeply?
He hates him, and if the chance arises, he will kill him! But on the
surface he will remain loyal—he has to. It is not out of joy, it is out
of fear. It is not out of love, it is out of a conditioned mind that says
you have to be loyal to your master. It is the loyalty of the dog to his
master.

Love needs a more total response. It comes not out of duty but out
of your own heartbeats, out of your own experience of joy, out of the
desire to share it. Loyalty is something ugly. But for thousands of years it
has been a very respectable value because society has enslaved people in
different ways. The wife is supposed to be loyal to the husband—to the
point that in India millions of women have died with their husband's
death, jumping onto the funeral pyre and burning to death. It was so respectable that any woman who would not do it had to live a very condemned life. She became almost an outcast; she was treated only as a

servant in her own family. It was concluded that because she could not die with her husband, she was not loyal to him.

In fact, just think of it the other way around: Not a single man has jumped onto his wife's funeral pyre! Nobody has raised the question, "Does that mean that no husband has ever been loyal to his wife?" But it is a society of double standards. One standard is for the master, the owner, the possessor, and the other standard is for the slave.

Love is a dangerous experience because you are possessed by something that is bigger than you. And it is not controllable; you cannot produce it on order. Once it is gone, there is no way to bring it back. All that you can do is to pretend, be a hypocrite.

Loyalty is a totally different matter. It is manufactured by your own mind, it is not something beyond you. It is a training in a particular culture, just like any other training. You start acting, and by and by you start believing your own acting. Loyalty demands that you should always, in life or in death, be devoted to the person whether your heart is willing for it or not. It is a psychological way of enslavement.

Love brings freedom. Loyalty brings slavery. On the surface they look alike; deep down, they are just the opposite, diametrically opposite. Loyalty is acting; you have been educated for it. Love is wild; its whole beauty is in its wildness. It comes like a breeze with great fragrance, fills your heart, and suddenly where there was a desert there is a garden full of flowers. But you don't know from where it comes, and you don't know that there is no way to bring it. It comes

> Love brings freedom. Loyalty brings slavery. On the surface they look alike, deep down, they are just the opposite.

on its own and remains as long as existence wills it. And just as it had come one day, as a stranger, as a guest, suddenly one day it is gone. There is no way to cling to it, no way to hold it.

Society cannot depend on such unpredictable, unreliable experiences. It wants guarantees, securities; hence it has removed love from life completely and it has put marriage in its place. Marriage knows loyalty, loyalty to the husband, and because it is formal, it is within your hands . . . but it is nothing compared to love—it is not even a dewdrop in the ocean that love is.

> Loyalty is acting, you have been educated for it. Love is wild, its whole beauty is in its wildness.

But society is very happy with it because it is reliable. The husband can trust you, trust that tomorrow, too, you will be as loyal as you are today. Love cannot be trusted—and the strangest phenomenon is that love is the greatest trust but it cannot be trusted. In the moment it is total, but the next moment remains open. It may grow within you; it may evaporate from you. The husband wants a wife who is a slave for her whole life. He cannot depend on love; he has to create something looking like love but manufactured by man's mind.

It is not only in the relationship of love but also in other fields of life that loyalty has been given great respect. But it destroys intelligence. The soldier has to be loyal to the nation. The man who dropped atom bombs on Hiroshima and Nagasaki—you cannot call him responsible; he was simply fulfilling his duty. He was ordered, and he was loyal to his superiors; that is the whole training of armies. For years they train you so that you become almost incapable of revolt. Even if you see that what is being asked from you is absolutely wrong, still your training has gone so deep you will say, "Yes, sir, I will do it."

I cannot conceive that the man who dropped the bombs on Hiroshima and Nagasaki was a machine. He also had a heart, just like you. He also had his wife and children, his old mother and father. He was as much a human being as you are—with a difference. He was trained to follow orders without questioning, and when the order was given, he simply followed it.

I have thought again and again about his mind. Is it conceivable that he did not think that this bomb would destroy almost two hundred thousand people? Could he not have said, "No! Is it not better to be shot by the general for not following the order than to kill two hundred thousand people"? Perhaps the idea never occurred to him.

The army works in such a way as to create loyalty; it starts with small things. One wonders why every soldier for years has to do parades and follow stupid orders—left turn, right turn, go backward, go forward—for hours, for no purpose at all. But there is a hidden purpose in it. His intelligence is being destroyed. He is being turned into an automaton, into a robot. So when the order comes, "Left turn," the mind does not ask why. If somebody else says to you, "Left turn," you are going to ask, "What nonsense is this? Why should I turn left? I'm

> The strangest phenomenon is that love is the greatest trust but it cannot be trusted. In the moment it is total, but the next moment remains open. It may grow within you, it may evaporate from you.

going right!" But the soldier is not supposed to doubt, to inquire; he simply has to follow. This is his basic conditioning for loyalty.

> It is comfortable for parents that their children are loyal because a child who is a rebel is a problem. The parents may be wrong, and the child may be right, but he has to be obedient.

It is good for the kings and for the generals that armies should be loyal to the point that they function like machines, not like men. It is comfortable for parents that their children are loyal because a child who is a rebel is a problem. The parents may be wrong, and the child may be right, but he has to be obedient to the parents; that is part of the training of the old man that has existed up to now.

I teach you the new human being in whom loyalty has no place but who has instead intelligence, inquiry, a capacity to say no. To me, unless you are capable of saying no, your yes is meaningless. Your yes is just recorded on a gramophone record; you cannot do anything, you have to say yes because the no simply does not arise in you.

Life and civilization would have been totally different if we had trained people to have more intelligence. So many wars would not have happened because people would have asked, "What is the reason? Why should we kill people, people who are innocent?" But they are loyal to one country and you are loyal to another country, and both the countries' politicians are fighting and sacrificing their people. If the politicians love to fight so much, they can have a wrestling match, and people can enjoy it just like any football match.

But the kings and the politicians, the presidents and the prime ministers don't go to war. The simple people, who have nothing to do with killing others, go to war to kill and to be killed. They are rewarded for their loyalty—they are given the Victoria Cross or other kinds of awards for being inhuman, for being unintelligent, for being mechanical.

> Unless you are capable of saying no, your yes is meaningless.

Loyalty is nothing but the combination of all these diseases—belief, duty, respectability. They all are nourishment for your ego. They are all against your spiritual growth, but they are in favor of the vested interests. The priests don't want you to ask any question about their belief system because they know that they have no answers to give. All belief systems are so false that if questioned, they will fall down. Unquestioned, they create great religions with millions of people in their folds.

Now, the pope has millions of people under him, and out of these millions of people, not a single one inquires, "How can a virgin girl give birth to a child?" That would be sacrilegious! Out of millions of people not a single one asks, "What is the evidence that Jesus is the only begotten Son of God? Anybody can claim it. What is the evidence that Jesus has saved people from misery? He could not save himself." But questions like these are embarrassing, and they are simply not raised. Even God is nothing but a hypothesis, which religious people have been trying to prove for thousands of years . . . all kinds of proofs but all bogus, with no substance, no support from existence. But nobody asks the question.

From the very first day of life people are being trained to be loyal to the belief system in which they were born. It is convenient for the priests to exploit you, it is convenient for the politicians to exploit you, it is convenient for husbands to exploit wives, for parents to exploit children, for teachers to exploit students. For every vested interest, loyalty is simply a necessity. But it reduces the whole of humanity into retardedness. It does not allow questioning. It does not allow doubt. It does not allow people to be intelligent. And a man who is not capable of doubting, of questioning, of saying "No" when he feels that the thing is wrong has fallen below humanity, has become a subhuman animal.

If love is asked, then it becomes loyalty. If love is given without being asked, it is your free gift. Then it raises your consciousness. If trust is asked, you are being enslaved. But if a trust arises in you, something superhuman is growing within your heart. The difference is very small but of tremendous importance: asked or ordered, love and trust both become false. When they arise on their own, they have immense intrinsic value. They do not make you a slave, they make you a master of yourself because it is your love, it is your trust. You are following your own heart. You are not following somebody else. You are not being forced to follow. Out of your freedom is your love. Out of your dignity is your trust—and they are both going to make you richer human beings.

That is my idea of the new humanity. People will love, but they will not allow love to be ordered. They will trust, but they will trust according to themselves—not according to any scriptures, not according to any social structure, not according to any priest, not according to any politician.

To live your life according to your own heart, following its beat, going into the unknown just like an eagle flying across the sun in utter freedom, knowing no limits . . . it is not ordered. It is its own joy. It is the exercise of one's own spirituality.

TOOLS FOR
TRANSFORMATION

This is one of the hardest truths to recognize, that one remains the same—that whatsoever we do, we remain the same. There is no "improvement." The whole ego is shattered because the ego lives through improvement, the idea of improvement, the idea of reaching somewhere someday. Maybe not today but tomorrow, or the day after tomorrow. To recognize the fact that there is no improvement in the world, that life is just a celebration, it has nothing like business in it—once you understand this, the whole ego trip stops, and suddenly you are thrown back to this moment.

ACCEPT YOURSELF

The moment you accept yourself you become open, you become vulnerable, you become receptive. The moment you accept yourself there is no need for any future because there is no need to improve upon anything. Then all is good, then all is good as it is. In that very experience life starts taking a new color, a new music arises.

If you accept yourself, that is the beginning of accepting all. If you reject yourself, you are basically rejecting the universe; if you reject yourself, you are rejecting existence. <u>If you accept yourself, you have accepted existence</u>; then there is nothing else to do but to enjoy, to celebrate. <u>There is no complaint left, there is no grudge; you feel grateful.</u> Then life is good and death is good, then joy is good and sadness is good, then to be with your beloved is good and to be alone is good. Then whatsoever happens is good because it happens out of the whole.

> ⤜
>
> Anxiety is the tense state between that which you are and that which you should be. People are bound to remain anxious if there is a "should" in life.

But you have been conditioned for centuries not to accept yourself. All the cultures of the world have been poisoning the human mind because they all depend on one thing: Improve yourself. <u>They all create anxiety in you</u>—anxiety is the tense state between that which you are and that which you should be. People are bound to remain anxious if there is a "should" in life. If there is an ideal that has to be fulfilled, how can you be at ease? How can you be at home? It is impossible to live anything totally because the mind is hankering for the future. And that future never comes—it cannot come. By the very nature of your desire it is impossible. When it comes you will start imagining other things, you will start desiring other things. You can always imagine a better state of affairs. And you can always remain in anxiety, tense, worried—that's how humanity has been living for centuries.

Only rarely, once in a while, has a man escaped out of the trap. That man is called a Buddha, a Christ. The awakened man is one who has slipped out of the trap of society, who has seen that this is just absurdity. You cannot improve yourself. And I am not saying that improvement does not happen, remember—but *you* cannot improve yourself. When you stop improving yourself, life improves you. In that relaxation, in that acceptance, life starts caressing you, life starts flowing through you. And when you don't have any grudge, any complaint, you bloom, you flower.

So I would like to say to you: Accept yourself as you are. And that is the most difficult thing in the world because it goes against your training, your education, your culture. From the very beginning you have been told how you should be. Nobody has ever told you that you are good as you are; they have all put programs in your mind. You have been programmed by parents, by priests, politicians, teachers—you have been programmed for only one thing: Just go on improving upon yourself. Wherever you are, go on rushing for something else. Never rest. Work unto death.

My teaching is simple: Don't postpone life. Don't wait for tomorrow, it never comes. Live it today!

Jesus says to his disciples "Look at the lilies in the field. They toil not, they weave not, they spin not—yet even Solomon was not so beautiful as these poor lily flowers." What is the beauty of the poor flower? It is in utter acceptance. It has no program in its being to improve. It is here now—dancing in the wind, taking a sunbath, talking to the clouds, falling asleep in the afternoon warmth, flirting with the butterflies . . . enjoying, being, loving, being loved.

> When you stop improving yourself, life improves you. In that relaxation, in that acceptance, life starts caressing you, life starts flowing through you.

And the whole existence starts pouring its energy into you when you are open. Then the trees are greener than they look to you now, then the sun is sunnier than it looks to you now; then everything becomes psychedelic, becomes colorful. Otherwise everything is drab and dull and gray.

Accept yourself—that is prayer. Accept yourself—that is gratitude. Relax into your being—this is the way God wanted you to be. In no other way did he want you to be; otherwise he would have made you somebody else. He has made you *you* and nobody else. Trying to improve upon yourself is basically trying to improve upon God— which is just stupid, and you will get madder and madder in trying that. You will not arrive anywhere, you will have simply missed a great opportunity.

> Life is not a miser, existence always gives abundantly—but we cannot receive it because we don't feel that we are worthy.

Let this be your color: acceptance. Let this be your characteristic: acceptance, utter acceptance. And then you will be surprised: Life is always ready to shower its gifts on you. Life is not a miser, existence always gives abundantly—but we cannot receive it because we don't feel that we are worthy to receive it.

That's why people cling to miseries— they suit their programming. People go on punishing themselves in a thousand and one subtle ways. Why? Because that fits with the program. If you are not as you should be, you have to punish yourself, you have to create misery for yourself. That's why people feel good when they are miserable.

Let me say it: People feel happy when they are miserable; they become very, very uneasy when they are happy. This is my observation of thousands and thousands of people: When they are miserable, every-thing is as it should be. They accept it—it fits with their conditioning, with their mind. They know how horrible they are, they know that they are sinners.

You have been told that you are born in sin. What stupidity! What non-sense! Man is not born in sin, man is born in innocence. There has never been any original sin, there has only been original innocence. Each child is born in innocence. We make him feel guilty—we start saying, "This should not be. You should be like this." And the child is nat-ural and innocent. We punish him for

> There has never been any original sin, there has only been original innocence. Each child is born in innocence.

being natural and innocent, and we reward him for being artificial and cunning. We reward him for being phony—all our rewards are for phony people. If somebody is innocent, we don't give any reward; we don't have any regard for him, we don't have any respect for him. The innocent is condemned, the innocent is thought to be almost synonymous with the criminal. The innocent is thought to be foolish, the cunning is thought to be intelligent. The phony is accepted—the phony fits with the phony society.

Then your whole life will be nothing but an effort to create more and more punishments for yourself. And whatsoever you do is wrong, so you have to punish yourself for every joy. Even when joy comes—in spite of yourself, mind you, when joy comes in spite of yourself, when sometimes God simply bumps into you and you cannot avoid him—immediately you start punishing yourself. Something has gone wrong—how can this happen to a horrible person like you?

Just the other night a man asked me, "You talk, Osho, about love,

> Even when joy comes,
> immediately you start
> punishing yourself.
> Something has gone
> wrong—how can this
> happen to a horrible
> person like you?

you talk of offering your love. But what have I got to give to anybody? What have I got to offer to my beloved?"

This is the secret idea of everybody: "I have nothing." What do you not have? But nobody has told you that you have all the beauties of all the flowers—because man is the greatest flower on this earth, the most evolved being. No bird can sing the song that you can sing—the birds' songs are just noises, although they are still beautiful because they come out of innocence. You can sing far better songs, of greater significance, of much more meaning. But you ask, "What have I got?"

The trees are green, beautiful, the stars are beautiful and the rivers are beautiful—but have you ever seen anything more beautiful than a human face? Have you ever come across anything more beautiful than human eyes? On the whole earth there is nothing more delicate than the human eyes—no rose can compete, no lotus can compete. And what depth! But you want to know, "What have I got to offer in love?" You must have lived a self-condemning life; you must have been putting yourself down, burdening yourself with guilt.

In fact, when somebody loves you, you are a little bit surprised. "What—*me?* A person loves *me?*" The idea arises in your mind: "Because he does not know me, that's why. If he comes to know me, if he comes to see through me, he will never love me." So lovers start hiding themselves from each other. They keep many things private, they don't open their secrets because they are afraid that the moment they open their heart, the love is bound to disappear—because they cannot love themselves, how can they conceive of anybody else loving them?

Love starts with self-love. Don't be selfish but be self-full—and they are two different things. Don't be a Narcissus, don't be obsessed with yourself. But a natural self-love is a must, a basic phenomenon. Only then out of it can you love somebody else.

Accept yourself, love yourself, you are God's creation. God's signature is on you, and you are special, unique. Nobody else has ever been like you, and nobody else will ever be like you—you are simply unique, incomparable. Accept this, love this, celebrate this—and in that very celebration you will start seeing the uniqueness of the others, the incomparable beauty of the others. Love is possible only when there is a deep acceptance of oneself, the other, the world. Acceptance creates the milieu in which love grows, the soil in which love blooms.

> Don't be selfish but be self-full—and they are two different things. Don't be a Narcissus, don't be obsessed with yourself. But a natural self-love is a must.

LET YOURSELF BE VULNERABLE

Lao Tzu says:

When man is born, he is tender and weak; at death, he is hard and stiff. When things and plants are alive, they are soft and supple; when they are dead, they are brittle and dry. Therefore hardness and

stiffness are the companions of death, and softness and gentleness are
the companions of life.

    Therefore when an army is headstrong, it will lose in battle.
When a tree is hard, it will be cut down. The big and strong belong
underneath. The gentle and weak belong at the top.

Life is a river, a flow, a continuum with no beginning and no
end. It is not going somewhere, it is always here. It is not going
from somewhere to somewhere else, it is always coming from here
to here. The only time for life is now, and the only place is here.
There is no struggle to reach, there is nothing to reach. There is no
struggle to conquer, there is nothing to conquer. There is no effort
to protect, because there is nothing to be protected from. Only life
exists, alone, absolutely alone, beautiful in its aloneness, majestic in
its aloneness.

You can live life in two ways: You can flow with it—then you
are also majestic, you have a grace, a grace of nonviolence, no conflict,
no struggle. Then you have a beauty, childlike, flowerlike, soft, delicate, uncorrupted. If you flow with life, you are religious. That's what
religion means to Lao Tzu, or to me.

Ordinarily religion means a fight with life, for God. Ordinarily it
means God is the goal, and life has to be denied and fought. Life has
to be sacrificed, and God has to be achieved. This ordinary religion is
no religion. This ordinary religion is just part of the ordinary, violent,
aggressive mind.

There is no God beyond life; life is God. If you deny life, you
deny God; if you sacrifice life, you sacrifice God. In all the sacrifices,
only God is sacrificed. George Gurdjieff used to say—it looks para-
doxical, but it is true—that all religions are against God. If life is God,
then to deny, to renounce, to sacrifice is to go against God. But it

seems Gurdjieff did not know much about Lao Tzu. Or even if he had known about Lao Tzu, he would have said the same thing because Lao Tzu does not seem to be ordinarily religious. He is more like a poet, a musician, an artist, a creator than a theologian, a priest, a preacher, philosopher. He is so ordinary that you cannot think that he is religious. But, really, to be religious is to be so extraordinarily ordinary in life that the part is not against the whole, but the part is flowing with the whole. To be religious is not to be separate from the flow.

To be irreligious is to have your own mind in an effort to win, to conquer, to reach somewhere. If you have a goal, you are irreligious. If you are thinking of the tomorrow, you have already missed religion. Religion has no tomorrow to it. That's why Jesus says, "Think not of the morrow. Look at the lilies in the field, they are blossoming now." Everything that is, is now. Everything that is alive is alive now. Now is the only time, the only eternity.

> If you have a goal, you are irreligious. If you are thinking of the tomorrow, you have already missed religion. Religion has no tomorrow to it.

There are two possibilities. One way is you can fight with life, you can have your private goals against life—and all goals are private, all goals are personal. You are trying to impose a pattern on life, something of your own. You are trying to drag life to follow you and you are just a tiny part, infinitesimal, so small, and you are trying to drag the whole universe with you. Of course you are bound to be defeated. You are bound to lose your grace, you are bound to become hard.

Fighting creates hardness. Just think of fight, and a subtle hardness comes around you. Just think of resisting, and a crust arises around you, which covers you like a cocoon. The very idea that you have a certain goal makes you an island; you are no longer part of the vast continent of life. And when you are separated from life, you are like a tree that is separated from the earth. It may live a little of the past nourishment, but really it is dying. The tree needs roots; the tree needs to be in the earth, joined with it, part of it.

> You need to be joined with the continent of life, part of it, rooted in it. When you are rooted in life, you are soft because you are not afraid.

You need to be joined with the continent of life, part of it, rooted in it. When you are rooted in life, you are soft because you are not afraid. Fear creates hardness. Fear creates the idea of security, fear creates the idea of protecting yourself. And nothing kills like fear because in the very idea of fear you are separated from the earth, uprooted.

Then you live on the past—that is why you think so much of the past. It is not coincidental. The mind continuously thinks either of the past or of the future. Why think so much of the past? The gone is gone! It cannot be recovered. The past is dead! Why do you go on thinking about the past, which is no more and about which nothing can be done? You cannot live it, you cannot be in it, but it can destroy your present moment. But there must be some deep-rooted cause for it. The deep-rooted cause is that you are fighting the whole. Fighting the whole, fighting the river of life, you are uprooted. You have become tiny, a capsulelike phenomenon, closed in yourself. You have become an individual, you are no longer part of the expanding universe, the vast. No, you are no longer part of it. You have to live like a miser on your past nourishment; that's why the mind goes on thinking about the past.

And you have to gather yourself somehow to be ready to fight; that's why you also go on thinking about the future. Future gives you hope, past gives you nourishment, and just between the two is eternity, the very life, which you are missing. Between the past and the future you are dying, not living.

There is another way to be—really, the only way to be because this way is not the way to be; the way of fight is not to be the way to be. The other way is to flow with the river, flow so together with it that you don't feel that you are separate and flowing with it. No, you become part of it—not only part, you are immersed in it; you have become the river, there exists no separation. When you are not fighting, you become life. When you are not fighting, you have become the vast, the infinite. In the East that state has been known as surrender, trust—what we have called *shraddha,* trusting life. Not trusting your individual mind but trusting the whole. Not trusting the part but the whole. Not trusting the mind but trusting existence. Surrendered, suddenly you become soft because then there is no need to be hard. You are not fighting, there is no enmity. There is no need to protect, there is no urge to be secure; you are already merged with life.

And life *is* secure! Only individual egos are insecure; they need protection, they need safety, they need armor around them. They are afraid, continuously trembling—then how can you live? You live in anguish and anxiety, you don't live. You lose all delight, the sheer joy of being here—and it is a sheer joy. It has no cause to it; it simply arises because you are. It simply bubbles up within you just because you are. Once you are open, flowing with life, you are bubbling with joy continuously, for no reason at all! You simply start feeling that to be is to be happy.

That's why Hindus have called the ultimate *satchitananda*—truth, consciousness, bliss. It means that to *be* is to be blissful, to be true is to be blissful. There is no other way of being. If you are miserable, that only shows that you have lost contact with being. To be miserable means somehow you are uprooted from the earth; you have become separate from the river, you have become a frozen block, an ice cube, floating in the river but not *with* it. Fighting, even trying to go upstream—the ego always wants to go upstream because wherever there is challenge, the ego feels good. The ego is always in search of fight. If you cannot find anybody to fight, you will feel very miserable. Somebody is needed to fight. In fighting you feel good, you *are*. But that is a pathological way, a neurotic way to be. Neurosis is fighting with the river. If you fight, you become hard. If you fight, you surround yourself with a dead wall. Of course, your own being is dead. You lose softness, lucidity, grace, gentleness. Then you are just dragging, not alive.

Lao Tzu is for surrender. He says, "Surrender to life. Allow life to lead you, don't try to lead life. Don't try to manipulate and control life, let life manipulate and control you. Let life possess you. You simply surrender, you simply say, 'I am not.' You give total power to life, and be with it."

It is difficult, because the ego says, "Then what am I? Surrendered, I am no more." But when the ego is not, in fact for the first time *you are*. For the first time you are not the finite, you are the infinite. For the first time you are not the body, the embodied, you are the unembodied, the vast, which goes on expanding—beginningless, endless.

But the ego does not know about it. The ego is afraid. It says,

"What are you doing, losing yourself? You will be lost, you will be a nobody." If you listen to the ego, the ego will put you again and again on a neurotic path, the path of being "somebody." And the more you become somebody, the more life has disappeared from you. Look at people who have succeeded in the world, who have become some-body, whose names are found in *Who's Who*. Look at them, watch them: You will find that they are living a fake life. They are only masks, nothing inside, hollow men—stuffed maybe, but not alive. Empty.

Watch people who have become successful in the world, who have become somebodies—presidents, prime ministers, the very rich—who have attained all that can be attained in the world. Watch them, touch them, look at them; you will feel death. You will not find throbbing hearts there. Maybe the heart is still beating, but the beat is mechanical. The beat has lost the poetry. They look at you, but their eyes are dull; the luster of being alive is not there. They will shake hands with you, but in their hands you will not feel anything flowing, you will not feel any exchange of energy, you will not see warmth welcoming you. A dead hand—weight you will find there, love you will not find. Look around them; they live in hell. They have succeeded, they have be-come somebodies, and now only hell surrounds them. You are on the same path if you are trying to be somebody.

Lao Tzu says, be a nobody, and then you will have infinite life flowing in you. For the flow of life, to be a somebody becomes a block. To be a nobody, a vast emptiness, allows all. Clouds can move, stars can move in it. And nothing disturbs it. And you have nothing to lose because all that can be lost you have surrendered already.

In such a state of being one is ever young. The body, of course, will become old, but the innermost core of your being remains young, fresh. It never becomes old, it is never dead. And Lao Tzu says this is the way to be really religious. Float with Tao, move with Tao, don't create any private goals and ends. The whole knows better; you are simply with it. The whole has created you, the whole breathes within you, the whole lives in you. Why do you bother? Let the responsibility be with the whole. You simply go wherever it leads. Don't try to force and plan, and don't ask for any certain goals because then there will be frustration, and you will become hard, and you will miss an opportunity of being alive.

And this is the point: If you allow life, more life happens. Then if you allow yourself to be alive, still more life happens. Jesus goes on saying, "Come to me, and I will show you the way of infinite life, life abundant. Life overflowing, flooding." But we live like beggars. We could have been like emperors, nobody else is responsible. Your cleverness to be yourself, to be clinging to the ego, is the whole cause of your misery.

Now the sutras:

When man is born, he is tender and weak.

Watch a small baby, just born. He has no crust around him. He is vulnerable, open, soft—life in its purity. It will not be so for long, soon personalities will start growing around him, he will be encaged, imprisoned by society, parents, schools, universities; soon life will become a distant phenomenon. He will be more like a prisoner. Life will go on beating somewhere deep inside him, but even he will not be able to hear the beat of it.

But when a child is born, watch it. Again and again the miracle happens. Again and again life goes on showing you the way, how to be, again and again life goes on saying that life is renewed every day. Old men die, new small babies are born. What is the point in it? It is very clear that life does not believe in oldness. In fact, if life were run by economists, this would seem to be very uneconomical, a wastage. An old man—trained, experienced in the ways of life and world— when he is ready, when he thinks he has become wise, death takes over and replaces the old man with a small baby with no knowledge, no wisdom at all, absolutely fresh, a tabula rasa; everything has to be written again. If you ask the economists, they will say this is foolish! God should consult economists first. What is he doing? It is a waste, sheer waste! A trained man of eighty dies, and an untrained babe is replacing him—this should be just the opposite; then it will be more economical.

But life does not believe in economics. And it is good that it doesn't believe, otherwise the whole world would have become a big cemetery. It believes in life, not in economics. It goes on replacing old people with the new, dead people with the young, hard people with the soft. The indication is clear: Life loves softness because through a soft being life can flow easily.

When man is born, he is tender and weak.

And Lao Tzu insists on the second point also: that life does not believe in strength. Weakness has a beauty in it because it is tender and soft. A storm comes; big, strong trees will fall. Small plants will simply bend, and then the storm goes by, and they are again smiling and flowering. In fact, the storm has freshened them, it has taken their dust, that's all. They are more alive, younger, fresher, and the storm has given them a

> A storm comes, big, strong trees will fall. Small plants will simply bend, and then the storm goes by, and they are again smiling and flowering.

good bath. And the old trees, very strong, have fallen because they resisted. They would not bend; they were very egoistic.

Lao Tzu says, "Life loves the weak." And that is the meaning of Jesus' saying, "Blessed are the meek because they shall inherit the earth. Blessed are the poor, the poor in spirit. Blessed are those who weep because they shall be comforted." Christianity goes on missing the meaning of Jesus' sayings because those sayings are Lao Tzuan. Unless they are related to Lao Tzu, they cannot be interpreted rightly. The whole teaching of Jesus is, "Be alive and be weak." That's why he says if somebody hits you on the face, give him the other side, too. If somebody takes your coat, give him your shirt, too. And if somebody forces you to walk with him for one mile, go for two miles. He is saying, "Be weak. Blessed are the meek."

What is there in weakness that is blessed? Because ordinarily the so-called leaders of the world, the teachers of the world, go on saying, "Be strong." And this Lao Tzu and this Jesus, they say, "Be weak." Weakness has something in it—because it is not hard. To be strong, one needs to be hard. To be hard, one needs to go against life. If you want to be strong, you will have to fight the flow; only then will you become strong. There is no other way to become strong. If you want to become strong, move upcurrent. The more the river forces you against it, the stronger you become. To be weak, flow with the river; wherever it is going, go with it. If the river says, "Go with me for one mile," go two miles. If the river takes your coat, also give your shirt. And if the river slaps you on one cheek, give the other.

Weakness has a certain beauty in it. The beauty is that of grace. The beauty is that of nonviolence, *ahimsa*. The beauty is that of love, forgiveness. The beauty is that of no conflict. And unless Lao Tzu is understood well and humanity starts feeling for Lao Tzu, humanity cannot live in peace.

If you are taught to be strong, you are bound to fight, wars will continue. All political leaders in the world go on saying that they love peace—and they all prepare for war. They say they stand for peace— and they all go on accumulating armaments. They talk about peace, and they prepare for war, and they all say they have to prepare for war because they are afraid of the other. And the other says the same thing! The whole thing looks so foolish and stupid. China is afraid of India, India is afraid of China. Why can't you see the point! Russia is afraid of America, Amer-

> ❧
>
> Weakness has a certain beauty in it. The beauty is that of grace. The beauty is that of nonviolence, love, forgiveness. The beauty is that of no conflict.

ica is afraid of Russia. They both talk about peace, and they both go on preparing for war. And, of course, that which you prepare for happens.

Your talk about peace looks like just rubbish. Your talk about peace is nothing but cold war. In fact, politicians need time to prepare—in that time they talk about peace so that they can have enough time to prepare. For centuries humanity has lived in only two periods: the period of war and the period of preparation for war. These are the only two periods. The whole history seems to be just neurotic.

But this is going to be so because strength is praised, ego is praised. If two persons are fighting on the road, one is stronger, another is weak—the weaker has fallen, and the stronger is sitting on his chest— whom do you appreciate? Do you appreciate the one who has become a conqueror? Then you are violent; then you are for war. Then you are a warmonger; then you are very dangerous and neurotic. Or do you appreciate the one who is weak? But nobody appreciates the weak;

> For centuries humanity has lived in only two periods: the period of war and the period of preparation for war. The whole of history seems to be just neurotic.

nobody wants to be associated with the weak because deep down you would also like to be strong.

When you appreciate the strong, you say, "Yes, this is my ideal; I would also like to be like him." If strength is praised, then violence is praised. If strength is praised, then death is praised because all strength kills—kills the other and also kills you. Strength is murderous and suicidal both.

Weakness—the very word seems to be condemnatory. But what is weakness? A flower is weak. A rock by the side of the flower is very strong. Would you like to be like a rock, or would you like to be like a flower? A flower is weak, remember, very weak— just a small wind and the flower will be gone. The petals will fall to the earth. A flower is a miracle; it is a miracle how the flower exists. So weak, so soft! Seems to be impossible—how is it possible? Rocks seem to be okay; they exist, they have their arithmetic to exist. But the flower? It seems to be completely unsupported—but still a flower exists; that's the miracle.

Would you like to be like a flower? If you ask, deep down your ego will say, "Be like a rock." And even if you insist, because a rock looks ugly, then the ego will say, "If you want to be a flower, be at least a plastic flower. Be at least strong! Winds won't disturb you, rains won't destroy you, and you can remain forever and ever." A real flower comes in the morning, laughs for a moment, spreads its fragrance, and is gone. An unreal flower, a plastic flower, can remain forever and

ever. But it is unreal, and it is strong because it is unreal. Reality is soft and
weak. And the higher the reality is, the
softer.

You cannot understand God because
your mind understands the logic of
rocks. You don't understand the logic of
a flower. Your mind can understand
mathematics. You don't have that aes-
thetic sense to feel for flowers. Only a
poetic mind can understand the possibility of God, because God is the weakest
and the softest. That's why it is the highest, it is the ultimate flower. It flowers,

> A real flower comes in the morning, laughs for a moment, spreads its fragrance, and is gone. An unreal flower, a plastic flower, can remain forever.

but it flowers only in a split second. That split second is known as
"the present." And it is such a small moment that you need to be
intensely attentive. Only then will you be able to see it; otherwise you
will miss it. It is always flowering—every moment it flowers, but you
cannot see because your mind is cluttered with the past and the future.
And the present is such a narrow phenomenon, just a flicker of the
eyelids and it is gone. In that narrow moment God flowers.

It is the highest, the ultimate. But it is very weak, very soft—it
has to be. It is the pinnacle, the last crescendo beyond which nothing exists. You will be able to understand God only when you understand the logic of softness and weakness. If you are trying to be
strong—conquerors, fighters, warriors—then you will live in the
world surrounded by rocks, not flowers, and God will be a faraway
phenomenon. It will not be possible for you to detect God anywhere in life.

When man is born, he is tender and weak; at death, he is hard and stiff.

So this should become your life: <u>Remain soft, tender, and weak</u>; don't try to be hard and stiff because that is how you are bringing your own death closer and closer. Death will come someday; that is not the point. Death is not the fear, death is not the problem. But if you are alive in a deathlike personality, that is the problem. Death in itself is very soft, softer than life, very tender. You can hear the sounds of life, but you cannot hear the sounds of death. When death comes, it is so soft that you cannot know even a second before that it is coming. And it is so weak, so tender, that death is not the problem. The death that you are living right now, that is the problem. Death before death is the problem; <u>living a dead life</u>, that is the problem. Hard, closed. Leibniz has a term for it. He calls it *monad*. *Monad* means closed in such a prison, in such a capsule, that there are no windows to look out of or for the outside to look in. A *monad* is an absolutely closed, windowless cell. *Monad* comes from the same root as monopoly, monastery, monk, and monogamy; it means to be totally alone. A monk is one who lives alone, a monastery is a place where people live alone. When you are completely closed, in a dead cell, you are in a monastery. You live in a cave by yourself, you cannot reach others, others cannot reach you. You are completely closed.

> Death will come some day; that is not the point. Death is not the fear, death is not the problem. But if you are alive in a deathlike personality, that is the problem.

This is the death that is stiff. And then you are miserable, and then you try to find ways and means how not to be miserable. You go on creating misery by being stiff, hard, and then you go on seeking methods how not to be miserable. In fact, if you understand the phenomenon of how you have become miserable, you can drop it immediately. Just be soft, flowing.

Be like a child, and always retain the purity and the softness of childhood. Don't lose contact with it, and you will be surprised one day when you discover that the child that you had been fifty years ago is still alive within you. If you know how to make contact with it, suddenly you are again a child.

The child is never lost because that is your life, it remains there. It is not that the child dies and then you become young, and then the youth dies, and then you become old, no. Layers upon layers accumulate, but the innermost core remains the same—the babe that you were born is still there within you; many layers have accumulated around it, and if you penetrate those layers, suddenly the child explodes in you. This explosion I have called ecstasy.

Jesus says, "Unless you become like children you will not enter the kingdom of God." This is what he means, and this is what I am talking about. If you penetrate your hard shell, the walls around you, the many layers, suddenly the child will explode within you. Again you will look at the world with those innocent eyes of a child. Then there is God.

God is not a very philosophical concept; it is this world looked at through the eyes of a child. The same world—these flowers, these trees, this sky, and

> God is not a very philosophical concept, it is this world looked at through the eyes of a child.

you—the same world suddenly takes on a new quality of being divine when you look at it through the eyes of a child. Only a pure, soft, tender heart is needed. God is not missing, *you* are missing. God is not absent, *you* are absent.

When man is born, he is tender and weak; at death, he is hard and stiff. When things and plants are alive, they are soft and supple; when they are dead, they are brittle and dry.

Learn. Life is teaching through many ways. Life is indicating the path how one should be.

Therefore hardness and stiffness are the companions of death, and softness and gentleness are the companions of life.

If you want to be more alive, abundantly alive, then seek companions of life: gentleness, softness.

All that clutters you makes you hard. Live in such a way that each moment you are free from the past moment. Your situation right now is like this: You have a big house with many rooms, and in all the rooms there are jigsaw puzzles. The whole house is filled with jigsaw puzzles—on the tables, on the chairs, on the beds, on the floors, hanging from the ceilings—everywhere jigsaw puzzles, and you have not been able to solve any. You try to solve one; feeling that to solve it is difficult, you move to another puzzle. But the first one is hanging on your head. Not only that,

> All that clutters you makes you hard. Live in such a way that each moment you are free from the past moment.

a few parts of it you carry with you to work on later on. Then you try to solve another puzzle, but you cannot solve it because you are yourself puzzled. Then you move to another room, and in this way you go on and on and on, in circles.

You are cluttered with unsolved puzzles, and by and by you are completely neurotic. Not a single point of life solved, and thousands of puzzles hanging around you. They take their toll. They kill you.

Never carry things on from the past—the past is gone. Every moment be rid of it, solved or not solved. Now nothing can be done about it. Drop it—and don't carry parts because those parts won't allow you to solve new problems that live in this moment. Live this moment as totally as possible, and suddenly you will come to realize that if you live it totally, it is solved. There is no need to solve it. Life is not a problem to be solved, it is a mystery to be lived. If you live it totally it is solved, and you come out of it beautiful, enriched, with new treasures of your being opened and nothing hanging around you. Then you move in another moment with that freshness, with this totality, intensity, so that another moment is lived and solved.

> Live this moment as totally as possible, and suddenly you will come to realize that if you live it totally, it is solved. There is no need to solve it. Life is not a problem to be solved, it is a mystery to be lived.

Never go on accumulating unlived moments around you; otherwise you will become hard. You can remain soft only if you don't carry anything from the past. Why are children soft? They don't carry anything. Their way is the way of the sage. If a child is angry, he is angry. In that moment he does not bother what Buddha says about anger. He does not bother with what Mahavira has taught about anger, "Don't be angry." He becomes really angry! He is so intensely angry that the very intensity becomes beautiful. Look at a child when he is really angry, the whole body—such a small body, so soft, so tender— throbbing with anger, eyes red, face red, jumping, screaming, as if he will destroy the whole world. An explosion of energy . . . And the next moment the anger is gone and he is playing, and look at his face— you cannot believe that this face was so angry a moment before. All smiles! So beautiful, so happy.

This is the way to live. One moment be in it, but be in it so totally that nothing is left over to be in another moment. The child lives the moment of anger; then he moves. When better education is possible in the world, we will not teach children not to be angry. We will teach them to be angry but *totally* angry—and not to carry it. Anger in itself is not bad. To carry it, to accumulate it, is dangerous. Flashes of anger are beautiful—in fact, necessary; they give a tone to life. They make life more salty. Otherwise you will feel flaccid; you won't have a tone. It is good exercise in itself, and if one can be in it totally and come out of it totally, unscratched, nothing is wrong in it.

> If you are not allowed to be angry, you become incomplete. You live the moment partially, the other parts hang on the mind. Then you are smiling but your smile is corrupted because that anger is hanging in it.

And a person who can be angry totally can be happy totally, can be loving totally because it is not a question of whether you are angry or happy or loving. The one thing you learn from all experiences is being total. If you are not allowed to be angry, you become incomplete. You live the moment partially, the other parts hang on the mind. Then you are smiling but your smile is not pure; it is corrupted because that anger is hanging in it. Your lips are smiling, but they are poisonous; the anger has not left, the past has not gone, you are not completely free to be here and now. The past has cast a shadow on you. And this goes on and on. You become puzzled. The whole of life becomes a hangover. Then you cannot live anything, you cannot love, you cannot pray, you cannot meditate.

People come to me and they say, "When we meditate, suddenly millions of thoughts arise. Ordinarily those thoughts are not arising, but when we meditate, then they arise." Why does it happen? Incomplete experiences—when you meditate you are unoccupied, and they all jump upon you: "You are unoccupied, at least solve us, complete us, fulfill us. You are not doing anything—meditation is not doing anything, just sitting here. Do something! This anger is there, resolve it. This love is there, fulfill it. This desire is there, do something!"

When you are occupied, you are so occupied that these things all surround you but never become the focus of your attention. But when you are meditating, they all try to attract your attention—"We are incomplete!" They are ghosts of your past.

Live every moment totally. And live with awareness, so that the past is not carried. And this is easy, just a little awareness is needed—nothing else is needed. Don't live in sleep, robotlike; be a little more conscious, and you will be able to see. And then you will become soft like a child, supple like a new, sprouting plant. And this quality can be carried to the very last moment of death; you remain supple. If you remain supple, young, fresh, death happens, but it does not happen to *you*. Because you carry life in you, death cannot happen. Only people

who have already been dead, die. People who have remained alive . . .
they watch death happening—the body dies, the mind dies, but not
them. They remain out of it, transcendental.

Therefore when an army is headstrong, it will lose in battle.

Lao Tzu looks absurd. He says when an army is headstrong it will
lose in battle, and you think whenever you are headstrong you will win.

*When a tree is hard, it will be cut down. The big and strong belong
underneath. The gentle and weak belong at the top.*

The roots are hard, they belong underneath. The flowers are soft,
they belong at the top. And this is the right structure of society: If the
people who are strong belong to the roots, and the people who are
soft belong to the top. Poets and painters should belong to the top.
Saints and sages should belong to the highest peak. Soldiers, politicians,
businessmen should belong underneath; they should not belong to the
top. The whole world is topsy-turvy because hard people are trying
to be on the top.

It is as if roots have become politicians, and they are trying to
come to the top of the tree, and they are trying to force the flowers
to go to the roots, to the underground. Once the world was more in
equilibrium—for example in India, the Brahmins belonged to the top.
We had placed them at the top. Brahmins are sages, those who have
known the *Brahma*. It is not a caste, it has nothing to do with birth;
it has to do with the inner resurrection. Those who have known the
ultimate are the Brahmans. They belonged to the top, they were the
flowers. Even kings, very strong emperors, had to come and bow down
at their feet. That was the right way—a king, howsoever strong and

howsoever great, is still a king. A man of the world is still neurotic, is still after ambition and ego; he has to bow down.

It happened:

Buddha was coming to a town, and the king of the town was a little hesitant to go and receive him. The prime minister, a very old, wise man, told the king, "You have to go." The king said, "This looks unnecessary. He is a beggar. Let him come! What is the point in me going to the boundary of my kingdom to receive him? I am a king, and he is a beggar."

The old prime minister wrote his resignation immediately. He said, "Take my resignation because if you have fallen so low, then I cannot remain here. You must remember that you are a king, and he has renounced kingdoms. He has nothing. You have a great empire, and he has nothing. He belongs to the top. And you have to go and bow down, otherwise take my resignation. I cannot be here in this palace with you. That is impossible for me." The king had to go.

When he bowed down to Buddha, Buddha said to him, "There was no need. I have heard that you were reluctant to come. There was no need because when one is reluctant, even if one comes, one does not come. And respect cannot be forced. Either you understand or you don't understand. There was no need—I was coming myself to see you. And I am a beggar . . . you are an emperor."

Now the king started crying and weeping. He understood the point.

In the East, Brahmans were on the top. That should be the right way to structure a society. Now all over the world politicians have

> All over the world, politicians have reached to the top. Hence the misery and the chaos—it has to be so. The top has become too heavy. Only flowers should be on the top—sages, poets, mystics. Not politicians.

reached to the top. Hence the misery and the chaos—it has to be so. The top has become too heavy. Only flowers should be on the top—sages, poets, mystics. Not politicians.

The big and strong belong underneath. The gentle and weak belong at the top.

Lao Tzu is saying that if you want to belong to the top, be gentle and weak. Be so weak and gentle, so soft like the grass, not strong like big trees.

Lao Tzu has a deep interest in all that is useless. He says to be useless is to be protected. To be useful is dangerous because if you are useful, then somebody is going to use you, you will be exploited. If you are strong, then you will be forced into the army.

Lao Tzu was passing through a village with his disciples and saw a man with a hunchback. He told his disciples, "Go to that hunchback and ask how he is feeling because I have heard the town has been in trouble. The king has forced all young men and strong men into the army."

They went to the hunchback and they asked him. The hunchback said, "I am happy! Because of my back, they didn't force me. I am useless. That's how I am saved." The disciples reported back. Lao Tzu said to them, "Now, remember. Be useless. Otherwise you will become fodder in the war."

Once passing through a forest they came under a huge tree; one thousand bullock carts could have rested underneath it. The whole forest was being cut down, thousands of carpenters were working there. Lao Tzu said, "Inquire what has happened—why have they not cut this big tree?"

The disciples went and inquired. The carpenter said, "That tree is absolutely useless. The branches are not straight, you cannot make furniture out of them—and when you burn it so much smoke comes out of it that it cannot be used as a fuel. And the leaves are so bitter that not even animals are ready to eat them. So it is useless. That is why we have not cut it down."

Lao Tzu started laughing and said to his disciples, "Be like that tree, useless. Then nobody will cut you down. And look at this tree, how big it has become, just by being useless!"

Life can be looked at in two ways. You can look at it as utilitarian: One thing has to be used for something else—then life becomes a means, and some end has to be fulfilled. Or life can be taken as enjoyment, not as a utility—then this moment is all, there is no goal, no purpose.

I was reading a poem just the other day. One line of it struck me deeply. "A poem should not mean, but be." I loved it. Life should not mean; life should be! An end in itself, going nowhere . . . enjoying here and now, celebrating. Only then can you be soft. If you are trying to be of use, you will become hard. If you are trying to achieve something, you will become hard. If you are trying to fight, you will become hard. Surrender. Be soft and tender. And allow the flow of life to take you wherever it takes you. Let the goal of the whole be your goal. Don't seek any private goal. Just be a part, and an infinite beauty and grace happens.

Try to feel it, what I am saying. It is not a question of understanding, it is not a question of intellectual capacity. Feel it, what I am saying. Imbibe it, what I am saying. Let it be there with you. Allow it to settle deep in your being: Life should not mean; life should be. And then suddenly you are soft. All hardness goes, disappears, melts. The baby is rediscovered; you have again become a child, those transparent eyes of childhood are available again. You can look, and then the greenery is totally different. The songs of the birds are totally different. Then the whole has a totally different significance. It has no meaning, it has significance. Meaning is concerned with utility; significance, with delight.

Delight in it and you will be soft. Flow with the river. Become the river.

BE SELFISH

Nobody can be unselfish except hypocrites.

The word *selfish* has taken on a very condemnatory association because all the religions have condemned it. They want you to be unselfish. But why? To help others. . . .

I am reminded:

A small child was talking to his mother, and the mother said, "Remember always to help others." And the child asked, "Then what will the others do?" Naturally the mother said, "They will help others." The child said, "This seems to be a strange scheme. Why not help yourself, rather than shifting it and making things unnecessarily complex?"

Selfishness is natural. Yes, there comes a moment when you are sharing by being selfish. When you are in a state of overflowing joy, then you can share. Right now miserable people are helping other miserable people, the blind leading others who are blind. What help can you give? It is a very dangerous idea, which has prevailed throughout the centuries.

> Miserable people are helping other miserable people, the blind leading others who are blind. What help can you give? It is a very dangerous idea.

In a small school the teacher told the boys, "At least once per week you should do a good thing." One boy asked, "Just please give us some examples of good things. We don't know what is good." So she said, "For example, a blind woman wants to cross the street; help her to cross the street. This is a good deed; this is virtuous."

The next week the teacher asked, "Did any of you remember to do what I have said to you?" Three children raised their hands. She said, "This is not good—almost the whole class has done nothing. But still, it is good that at least three boys did something good." She asked the first, "What have you done?" He said, "Exactly what you have said: One old woman who was blind, I helped her to cross the street."

She said, "That's very good. God will bless you." She asked the second, "What have you done?" He said, "The

same—a blind old woman, I helped her to cross the street."
The teacher became a little puzzled. Where are they finding
all these blind old women? But it was a big city; it was possible
they had found two. She asked the third, and he said, "I did
exactly what they have done: helped a blind old woman cross
the street."

The teacher asked, "But where did you find three blind
women?" They said, "You don't understand—there were not
three blind women, there was only one blind woman. And it
was so hard to help her to cross the street! She was beating us
and shouting and screaming because she did not want to cross.
But we were intent on doing some virtuous act, even though
a crowd gathered, people were shouting at us. But we said,
'Don't be worried. We are taking her to the other side.'"

People are being told to help others, and they are empty within
themselves. They are being told to love others—love your neighbors,
love your enemies—and they are never
told to love themselves. All the religions,
directly or indirectly, are telling people to
hate themselves. A person who hates
himself cannot love anybody; he can
only pretend.

The basic thing is to love yourself so
totally that the love overflows you and
reaches to others. I am not against sharing, but I am absolutely against altruism.
I am for sharing, but first you must have
something to share. And then you are
not doing anything as an obligation to

> I am not against
> sharing, but I am
> absolutely against
> altruism. I am for
> sharing, but first you
> must have something
> to share.

anybody—on the contrary, the person who receives something from you is obliging you. You should be thankful because the other could have rejected your help; the other has been generous.

My whole insistence is that the individual should be so happy, so blissful, so silent, so content that out of his state of fulfillment he starts sharing. He has so much, he is like a rain cloud—he has to shower. If others' thirst is quenched, if the thirst of the earth is quenched, that is secondary. If each individual is full of joy, full of light, full of silence, he will be sharing it without anyone telling him because sharing is such a joy. Giving it to someone is more joyful than getting it.

But the whole structure should be changed. People should not be told to be altruistic. They are miserable—what can they do? They are blind—what can they do? They have missed their life—what can they do? They can give only what they have. So people are giving misery, suffering, anguish, anxiety to everybody else who comes in contact with them. This is altruism? No, I would like everybody to be utterly selfish.

Each tree is selfish: It brings water to its roots, it brings juices to its branches, to the leaves, to the fruits, to the flowers. And when it blossoms, it releases fragrance to everybody—known, unknown, familiar, stranger. When it is loaded with fruits, it shares, it gives those fruits. But if you teach these trees to be altruistic, all these trees will die, just as the whole of humanity is dead—just corpses walking. And walking to where? Walking to their graveyard, finally to rest in their graves.

Life should be a dance. And everybody's life can be a dance. It should be music—and then you can share; you will have to share. I don't have to say it because this is one of the fundamental laws of existence: The more you share your bliss, the more it grows.

But I teach selfishness.

A MEDITATION TECHNIQUE

This method, and many similar methods, appear in
The Book of Secrets by Osho.

*Feel the consciousness of each person as your own consciousness. So,
leaving aside concern for self, become each being.*

Feel the consciousness of each person as your own consciousness—
in reality it is so, but it is not felt so. You feel your consciousness as
yours, and others' consciousnesses you never feel. At the most you
infer that others are also conscious. You infer that because you are
conscious, other beings like you must be conscious. This is a logical
inference; you don't feel them as conscious. It is just like when you
have a headache, you feel your headache, you have a consciousness of
it. But if someone else has a headache, you cannot feel the other's
headache. You simply infer that whatsoever he is saying must be true,
and he must have something like you. But you cannot feel it.

The feeling can come only if you become conscious about others'
consciousnesses—otherwise it is a logical inference. You believe, you
trust, that others are saying something honestly, and whatsoever they
are saying is worth believing because you have similar types of experiences.

There is a logical school that says nothing can be known about
the other, it is impossible. At the most there can be an inference, but
nothing certain can be known about others. How can you know
that others have pain like you, that others have anxieties like you?
Others are there, but we cannot penetrate them, we can only just

touch their surface. Their inner being remains unknown. We remain closed in ourselves.

The world around us is not a felt world, it is just inferred—logically, rationally. The mind says it is there, but the heart is not touched by it. That is why we behave with others as if they are things not persons. Our relationship with persons is also as it is with things. A husband behaves toward his wife as if she is a thing: He possesses her. The wife possesses the husband just like a thing. If we behaved with the other as if they were persons, then we would not try to possess them because only things can be possessed.

A person means freedom. A person cannot be possessed. If you try to possess them, you will kill them, they will become things. Our relationship with others is really not an "I-thou" relationship; deep down it is just an "I-it" relationship. The other is just a thing to be manipulated, to be used, exploited. That is why love becomes more and more impossible—because love means taking the other as a person, as a conscious being, as a freedom, as something as valuable as you are.

> A person cannot be possessed. If you try to possess them, you will kill them, they will become things.

If you behave as if everything is a thing, then you are the center, and things are just to be used. The relationship becomes utilitarian. Things have no value in themselves—the value is that you can use them, they exist for you. You can be related to your house—the house exists for you. It is a utility. The car exists for you, but the wife doesn't exist for you, and the husband doesn't exist for you. The husband exists for himself, and the wife exists for herself. A person exists for himself; that is what being a person means. And if you allow the person to be a person and don't reduce him to being a thing, you will by and by start feeling him. Otherwise you cannot feel. Your relationship will remain conceptual, intellectual, mind to mind, head to head—but not heart to heart.

This technique says: *Feel the consciousness of each person as your own consciousness.* This will be difficult because first you have to feel the person as a person, as a conscious being. Even that is difficult.

Jesus says, "Love your neighbor as you love yourself." This is the same thing—but the other must first become a person for you. He must exist in his own right, not to be exploited, manipulated, utilized, not as a means but as an end in himself. First, the other must become a person; the other must become a "thou," as valuable as you are. Only then can this technique be applied. *Feel the consciousness of each person as your own consciousness.* First feel that the other is conscious, and then this can happen—you can feel that the other has the same consciousness that you have.

> First, the other must become a person; the other must become a "thou," as valuable as you are. Only then can this technique be applied.

Really, the "other" disappears, only a consciousness flows between you and him. You become two poles of one consciousness flowing, of one current.

In deep love it happens that the two persons are not two. Something between the two has come into being, and they have just become two poles. Something is flowing between the two. When this flow is there, you will feel blissful. If love gives bliss, it gives bliss only because of this: that two persons, just for a single moment, lose their egos. The "other" is lost, and oneness comes into being just for a sin-

Tools for Transformation

gle moment. If it happens, it is ecstatic, it is blissful, you have entered paradise. Just a single moment, and it can be transforming.

This technique says that you can do this with every person. In love you can do it with one person, but in meditation you have to do it with every person. Whosoever comes near you, simply dissolve into him and feel that you are not two lives but one life, flowing. This is just changing the gestalt. Once you know how, once you have done it, it is very easy. In the beginning it seems impossible because we are so stuck in our own egos. It is difficult to lose it, difficult to become a flow. So it will be good if in the beginning you try with something that you are not very scared or afraid of.

You will be less afraid of a tree, so it will be easier. Sitting near a tree, just feel the tree, and feel that you have become one with it, that there is a flow within you, a communication, a dialogue, a melting. Sitting near a flowing river, just feel the flow, feel that you and the river have become one. Lying under the sky, just feel that you and the sky have become one. In the beginning it will be just imagination, but by and by you will feel that you are touching reality through imagination.

And then try it with persons. This is difficult in the beginning because there is a fear. Because you have been reducing persons to things, you are afraid that if you allow someone to be so intimate, he will also reduce you to a thing. That is the fear. So no one allows much intimacy: A gap is always to be kept and guarded. Too much closeness is dangerous because the other can convert you into a thing, he can try to possess you. That is the fear. You are trying to convert others into things, and others are trying to convert you—and no one wants to be a thing, no one wants to become a means, no one wants to be used. It is the most degrading phenomenon to be reduced to just a means to something, not valuable in yourself. But everyone is

135

> Too much closeness is dangerous because the other can convert you into a thing, he can try to possess you. That is the fear.

trying. Because of this there is a deep fear and it will be difficult to start this technique with persons.

So start with a river, with a hill, with the stars, with the sky, with trees. Once you come to know the feeling of what happens when you become one with the tree; once you come to know how blissful you become when you become one with the river, how without losing anything you gain the whole existence, then you can try it with people. And if it is so blissful with a tree, with a river, you cannot imagine how much more blissful it will be with a person, because a person is a higher phenomenon, a more highly evolved being. Through a person you can reach higher peaks of experience. If you can become ecstatic with even a rock, with a person you can feel a divine ecstasy happening to you.

But start with something that you are not much afraid of, or with a person you love—a friend, a beloved, a lover—of whom you are not afraid, with whom you can be really intimate and close without any fear, with whom you can lose yourself without getting scared deep down that he may turn you into a thing. If you have someone like that, then try this technique. Lose yourself consciously into him. When you lose yourself consciously into someone, that someone will lose himself into you; when you are open and you flow into the other, the other starts flowing into you and there is a deep meeting, a communion. Two energies melt into each other. In that state there is no ego, no individual—simply consciousness. And if this is possible with one individual, it is possible with the whole universe. What saints have called ecstasy, *samadhi,* is just a deep love phenomenon between a person and the whole universe.

Feel the consciousness of each person as your own consciousness. So, leaving aside concern for self, become each being. Become the tree, become the river, become the wife, become the husband, become the child, become the mother, become the friend—it can be practiced every moment of life. But in the beginning it will be difficult. So do it for at least one hour every day. In that hour, whatsoever passes around you, become that. You will wonder how it can happen—there is no other way to know how it can happen, you have to practice it.

Sit with the tree, and feel that you have become the tree. And when the wind comes and the whole tree starts shaking and trembling, feel that shaking and trembling in you; when the sun rises and the whole tree becomes alive, feel that aliveness in you; when a shower of rain comes and the whole tree is satisfied and content, a long thirst, a long awaiting has disappeared, and the tree is completely satisfied and content, feel satisfied and content with the tree, and then you will become aware of the subtle moods, of the nuances of a tree.

You have seen that tree for many years, but you don't know its moods. Sometimes it is happy; sometimes it is unhappy. Sometimes it is sad, worried, frustrated; sometimes it is very blissful, ecstatic. There are moods. The tree is alive, and it feels. And if you become one with it, then you will feel it. Then you will feel whether the tree is young or old; whether the tree is dissatisfied with its life or satisfied; whether the tree is in love with existence or not—is anti, against, furious, angry; whether the tree is violent or there is a deep compassion in it. As you are changing every moment, the tree is also changing—if you can feel a deep affinity with it, an empathy.

Empathy means you have become so sympathetic that, really, you become one. The moods of the tree become your moods. And then if this goes deeper and deeper and deeper, you can talk, you can have a communication with the tree. Once you know its moods, you start understanding its language, and the tree will share its mind with you. It will share its agonies and ecstasies.

And this can happen with the whole universe.

For at least one hour every day try to be in empathy with something. In the beginning you will look foolish to yourself. You will think, "What kind of stupidity am I doing?" You will look around, and you will feel that if someone looks or someone sees or someone comes to know, they will think you have gone crazy. But only in the beginning. Once you enter this world of empathy, the whole world will look crazy to you. They are missing so much unnecessarily. Life gives in such abundance and they are missing it. They are missing because they are closed: They don't allow life to enter into them. And life can enter you only if you enter life through many, many ways, through many paths, through multidimensions, Be in empathy for at least one hour every day.

This was the meaning of prayer in the beginning of every religion. The meaning of prayer was to be in an affinity with the universe, to be in a deep communication with the universe. In prayer you are talking to God—God means the totality. Sometimes you may be angry with God, sometimes thankful,

> Our prayers have gone rotten because we don't know how to communicate with beings. And if you cannot communicate with beings, you cannot communicate with Being—Being with a capital *B*—it is impossible.

but one thing is certain: You are in communication. God is not a mental concept, it has become a deep, intimate
relationship. That is what prayer means.

But our prayers have gone rotten
because we don't know how to communicate with beings. And if you cannot communicate with beings, you
cannot communicate with Being—Being with a capital *B*—it is impossible. If
you cannot communicate with a tree,
how can you communicate with the total existence? And if you feel foolish
talking to a tree, you will feel more
foolish talking to God.

> This was the meaning of prayer in the beginning of every religion. The meaning of prayer was to be in an affinity with the universe, to be in a deep communication with the universe.

Leave one hour aside every day for a prayerful state of mind, and
don't make your prayer a verbal affair. Make it a feeling thing. Rather
than talking with the head, feel it. Go and touch the tree, hug the
tree, kiss the tree; close your eyes and be with the tree as if you are
with your beloved. Feel it. And soon you will come to a deep understanding of what it means to put the self aside, of what it means to
become the other.

*Feel the consciousness of each person as your own consciousness. So, leaving
aside concern for self, become each being.*

ON THE WAY TO INTIMACY
RESPONSES TO QUESTIONS

People ask questions that make them feel very knowledgeable. They want to ask questions not to get the answer, but just to show their knowledge. But I am a crazy person: I never answer those questions that come out of your knowledge. I simply throw them away.

I only answer questions that open up your wounds because once your wounds are open, there is a possibility of healing. Once you expose yourself, you are on the way of transformation. And unless you show your real face, it is impossible to make any changes in your life, any transformations in your consciousness.

Why do I find attractive people frightening?

Attractive people are frightening for many reasons. First, the more attractive a person is to you, the more there is the possibility of falling into her or his bondage—that is the fear. You will be possessed, you will be reduced to a slave by the charm, the magnetism, the magic.

Attractive people *are* attracting and yet frightening. They are beautiful; you would like to relate with them, but to relate with them means to lose your freedom. To relate with them means not to be yourself anymore. And because they are attractive, you will not be able to leave them; you will cling. You know your tendency—that the more attractive a person is, the more clinging will arise in you; you will become more and more dependent. That is the fear.

Nobody wants to become dependent. Freedom is the ultimate value. Even love is not higher than freedom. Freedom is the ultimate value; next to it is love. And there is a constant conflict between love and freedom. Love tries to become the ultimate value. It is not. And love tries to destroy freedom; only then can it be the ultimate value. And those who love freedom become afraid of love.

And love means to be attracted to an attractive person. And the more beautiful the person is, the more you feel attracted, the more fear will arise because now you are going into something from where escape will not be easy. You can escape from an ordinary person, a homely person, more easily. And if the person is ugly, you are free; you need not become too dependent.

Mulla Nasruddin married the ugliest woman in the town. Nobody could believe it. People asked him, "Nasruddin, what has happened to you?"

He said, "There is a logic in it. This is the only woman from whom I can escape any time. In fact, it will be difficult not to escape. This is the only woman in the town whom I can trust. Beautiful people are not trustworthy. They can fall in love easily because so many people are attracted to them. I can trust this woman; she will always be sincere toward me. I need not be worried about her; I can go out of town for months; I will not have any fear. My woman will remain mine."

Just see the point: If the person is ugly, you can possess the person. The ugly person will depend on you. If the person is beautiful, the beautiful person will possess you. Beauty is power, it is tremendous power.

The ugly person will become a slave, a servant. The ugly person will in every way substitute for the beauty that is missing in him or her. The ugly woman will be a better wife than a beautiful woman— she will have to be. She will take more care of you, she will be a better nurse—because she knows that beauty is missing and something has to be provided instead. She will be very good to you; she will never nag you, she will never fight with you, she will not be in a constant quarrel with you—she cannot afford it.

Beautiful persons are dangerous. They can afford to fight. So these are the reasons.

You ask me, "Why do I find attractive people frightening?"

They are. Unless you understand and become aware, this fear remains. Attraction/fear are two aspects of the same phenomenon. You are always attracted to the same person with whom you feel a great fear. Fear means you will be secondary.

In fact, people want the impossible. A woman wants a man, the most beautiful, the most powerful man in the world—but also wants him to remain interested only in her. Now, this is an impossible demand. The most beautiful and the most powerful person is bound to be interested in many more people. And many more people will be interested in him. The man would like to have the most beautiful woman in the world, but also would like her to remain very faithful to him, devoted to him. That will be difficult; that is asking the impossible.

And remember: If some woman looks very beautiful to you, that simply shows you are not very beautiful. And you are afraid also—if the woman looks so beautiful to you, what is happening from the other side? You will not be looking so beautiful to her. There is fear—she may leave you. All these problems are there. But these problems arise only because your love is not really love but a game. If it is really love, then it never thinks of the future. Then there is no problem of the future. Tomorrow does not exist for real love; time does not exist for real love.

If you love a person, you love a person. What will happen to-morrow—who cares? Today is so much, this moment is an eternity. What will happen tomorrow, we will see . . . when tomorrow comes. And tomorrow never comes. Real love is of the present.

Always remember: Anything real has to be part of awareness, has to be part of the present, has to be part of meditation. Then there is no problem! And there is no question of attraction, and there is no question of fear.

Real love shares; it is not to exploit the other, it is not to possess the other. When you want to possess the other, then the problem arises: The other may possess you. And if the other is more powerful, more magnetic, naturally you will be a slave. If you want to become the master of the other, then the fear arises that "I may be reduced to a slave." If you don't want to possess the other, then the fear never arises that the other may possess you. Love never possesses.

Love never possesses and love can never be possessed. True love leads you into freedom. Freedom is the highest peak, the ultimate value. And love is closest to freedom; the next step after love is freedom. Love is not against freedom; love is a stepping-stone toward freedom. That's what awareness will make clear to you: that love has to be used as a stepping-stone for freedom. If you love, you make the other free. And when you make the other free, you are made free by the other.

Love is a sharing, not an exploitation. And in fact love never thinks in terms of ugliness and beauty, either. You will be surprised: Love never thinks in terms of ugliness and beauty. Love only acts, reflects, meditates—it never thinks at all. Yes, sometimes it happens that you fit with somebody—suddenly, everything falls in harmony. It is not a question of beauty or ugliness. It is a question of harmony, a rhythm.

Somebody has asked a question about what George Gurdjieff used to say, that for every man there is a corresponding woman somewhere on the earth, and for every woman there is a corresponding man somewhere on the earth. Each one is born with the polar opposite. If you can find the other, everything will fall in harmony immediately. All their centers function harmoniously—that is love. It is a very rare phenomenon. It is very rare to find a couple who really fit together. Our society exists with such taboos, such inhibitions, that it is almost impossible to find the real mate, the real friend.

In Eastern mythology we have a story, a beautiful myth, that in the beginning when the world was created, each child was born not alone but as a couple: one boy, one girl, together, from the same mother. Twins, fitting with each other totally—that was the couple. They were in tune in every way with each other. Then man fell from grace—just like the idea of the original sin—and as a punishment couples were no longer born from the same mother. Still, they are born! Gurdjieff is right—that's my own observation, too. Each person has a divine mate somewhere. But to find them is very difficult because you may be white and your opposite polarity may be black; you may be a Hindu and your opposite polarity may be a Mohammedan; you may be Chinese and the opposite polarity may be German.

In a better world, people will search and seek—and unless you can find the real person who can fit with you, you will remain in a kind of tension, anguish. If you are alone you are in anguish; if you meet the other person, you are in anguish if the other person does not fit with you or only fits so far. Now, through scientific investigation this has also been found: that there are people who fit, and there are people who don't fit. Scientific arrangements can be made now; each person can declare his centers, his birth chart, his rhythm. Now there is every possibility to find the other person who fits exactly. The world has become very small, and once you have found the other person . . . it is not a question of beauty and ugliness at all.

In fact, there is nobody who is ugly and nobody who is beautiful. The ugly person may fit with somebody—then the ugly person is beautiful for that person. Beauty is a shadow of harmony. It is not that you fall in love with a beautiful person; the process is just the opposite. When you fall in love with some person, the person looks beautiful. It is love that brings the idea of beauty in, not vice versa.

But it is rare to find a person who totally fits with you. Whenever somebody is fortunate enough, life is lived with a melody; then there are two bodies and one soul. That is a real couple. And whenever you can find that kind of couple, there will be great grace and great music around them, a great aura, beautiful light, a silence. And love then naturally leads into meditation.

People should be allowed to meet and mix to find each other. People should not be in a hurry to get married. The hurry is dangerous; it only brings divorces, or it brings a life of long, long misery. Children should be allowed to meet with each other, and we should drop all pre-technological taboos, inhibitions; they are no longer relevant.

We are living in a post-technological age; man has become mature, and he has to change many things because many things are wrong. They were developed in the old days; it was a necessity then—it is no longer a necessity. For example, now people can live together, men and women; there is no need to be in a hurry to get married. And if you have known many men and many women, only then will you know who fits with you and who does not fit. It is not a question of a long nose or a beautiful face; somebody may have a beautiful face and you feel attracted, and may have beautiful eyes and big eyes and you feel attracted, and the color of the hair . . . but these things don't matter! When you live together, after two days you will not note the color of the hair, and after three days you will not note the length of the nose; and after three weeks you will have completely forgotten about the physiology of the other. Now the reality impinges upon you. Now the real thing will be spiritual harmony.

Marriage up to now has been a very ugly affair. And priests were happy to allow it—not only happy to allow it, they were the ones who invented it. And there was some reason why priests all over the world have been in favor of this ugly marriage that has been on the earth for five thousand years. The reason was that if people are miserable, only then do they go to the churches, to the temples; if people are miserable, only then are they ready to renounce life. If people are miserable, only then are they in the hands of the priests! A happy humanity will have nothing to do with the priests. Obviously. If you are healthy, you have nothing to do with the doctor. If you are psychologically whole, you have nothing to do with the psychoanalyst. If you are spiritually whole, you will have nothing to do with the priest.

And the greatest spiritual disharmony is created by marriage. Priests have created hell on the earth. That is their trade secret—then people are bound to come to ask them what to do. Life is so miserable! And then they can tell them how to get free of life. Then they can give you rituals for how never to be born again, how to get out of the wheel of birth and death. They have made life such a hell, and then they teach you how to get rid of it.

My effort is just the opposite: I want to create heaven here now so that there is no need to get rid of anything. There is no need to think of getting rid of birth and death, and there is no need for the old so-called religions. More music is needed, more poetry is needed, more art is needed. Certainly more mysticism is needed. More science is needed. And then there will be a totally different kind of religion born, a new religion. A religion that will not teach you antilife ideologies but will help you to live your life in more harmony, more artistically, more sensitively, more centered, rooted in the earth. A religion that will teach you the art of life, the philosophy of life, and will teach you how to be more festive.

You ask, "Why do I find attractive people frightening?"

Because deep down in you there is a search, as there is in everybody, for the other pole, and you don't want to get involved with somebody who may not be the other pole. But there is no other way to find the other pole except by getting involved in many, many friendships, in many, many love affairs. If you really want to find your beloved, you will have to go through many love affairs. That is the only way to learn. Drop your fear. . . .

And if you start associating with ugly people out of your fear of beautiful people, that is not going to be satisfying to you.

The Cohens were renting a furnished apartment. Mr. Cohen had found the place, which met with all his requirements, but Mrs. Cohen demurred: "I don't like this flat."

"What's the matter, Rachel? Ain't it a fine flat? Why, it has all the latest improvements: washstands, decent lights, good plumbing, and hot and cold water. Why not?"

"I know all what you say, but there are no curtains in the bathroom. Every time I take a bath, the neighbors can see me."

"That's all right, Rachel. If the neighbors see you, *they* will buy the curtains."

Ugliness can have its uses, but it will not give you contentment. And if you are afraid of beautiful people, then remember that you are really afraid of getting involved in a deep, intimate relationship—that you want to keep a distance, that you want to keep a distance so you can escape any time if the need arises. But this is not the way to go into it; this is not the way to know the secrets of love. One has to go in absolute vulnerability. One has to drop all armor and defense.

If it is frightening, let it be frightening, but go into it. The fear will disappear. The only way to drop any fear is to go into the very thing of which you are afraid. If somebody comes to me and says, "I am afraid of darkness," then I always suggest to them, "The only way is to go into the dark night, sit somewhere alone outside the town under a tree. Tremble! Perspire, be nervous, but sit there! How long can you tremble? Slowly, slowly things will settle. The heart will start beating normally . . . and suddenly you will see that darkness is not that frightening, either. And slowly, slowly you will become aware of the beauties of darkness, which only darkness can have—the depth, the silence, the velvety touch of it, the stillness, the music of the dark night, the insects, the harmony. And slowly, as the fear disappears, you will be surprised that darkness is not that dark, it has its own luminosity. You will be able to start seeing something—vague, not clear. But clarity gives shallowness to things; vagueness gives depth and mystery. Light can never be so mysterious as darkness. Light is prose; darkness is poetry. Light is naked; hence, how long can you remain interested in it? But darkness is veiled; it provokes great interest, great curiosity, to unveil it.

If you are afraid of darkness, go into darkness. If you are afraid of love, go into love. If you are afraid of being alone, then go into the Himalayas and be alone. That is the only way to drop it. And sometimes if you can deliberately do something, it brings great awareness.

Once a young man was brought to me—he was a professor in a college—and the problem was that he walked like a woman. And to be in a university and to be a professor and to walk like a woman is troublesome. He was very much embarrassed. And he had tried all kinds of methods.

I said, "Do one thing—because this is impossible, what you are doing; a man cannot really walk like a woman. You are doing something like a miracle! Because to walk like a woman means you have to have a womb in your belly; it is because of that roundness of the womb that the woman walks in a different way. Her alignment of the body is different. But a man really cannot walk like that—if a man can do it . . ." I told him, "This should be something to be proud of! You are doing a miracle. Just show it to me."

He said, "What do you mean, a miracle?"

I said, "Just walk here in front of me, and walk like a woman."

He tried and he failed. He could not walk like a woman. And I told him, "Now, this is the key. Go back to the university—up to now you have been trying *not* to walk like a woman. From now on try to walk like a woman with every deliberate effort. Your effort *not* to walk like a woman has been the cause of the whole problem. It has become an obsession, a hypnosis. You have hypnotized yourself. The only way to dehypnotize yourself is to do it deliberately. Go to the university immediately," I told him, "and walk around, and try in every possible way to show that you are a woman."

He tried and he failed—and since then he has not succeeded.

If you are afraid, remember that it is the same whether you are afraid of attractive people or that nobody should touch your navel, or you are afraid of darkness, or you are afraid of walking like a woman, or you are afraid of this or that, XYZ, it doesn't matter. Fear has to be dissolved because fear is a crippling process, a paralyzing process.

And the only way to dissolve it is to go into it. Experience liberates. It is better to learn. It is better to drop fear. It is better to relate with people. And, in fact, if you start relating, you will find every person has something beautiful in her or him. Nobody comes without beauty. Maybe beauty has different dimensions—somebody's face is beautiful, somebody's voice is beautiful, somebody's body is beautiful, somebody's mind is beautiful. Nobody comes without beauty; existence gives to everybody some kind of beauty or other. There are as many beauties as there are people.

And the only way to contact the beauty of a person is to become intimate, to drop all fear, to drop all defenses. And you will be surprised: God is expressed in different forms—God is beauty.

We have three words for God in the East: *satyam*—truth, *shivam*—the ultimate good, *sundram*—the ultimate beauty. And beauty is the last—God is beautiful, God is beauty. Wherever you find beauty, it is a reflection of God's beauty. And if you are afraid of the reflection, how will you relate with the real? The reflection is there to learn the lesson so that one day you can relate with the real.

Why do I feel self-conscious?

Freedom is the goal of life. Without freedom, life has no meaning at all. By *freedom* is not meant any political, social, or economic freedom. By *freedom* it is meant freedom from time, freedom from mind, freedom from desire. The moment the mind is no more, you are one with the universe; you are as vast as the universe itself.

It is the mind that is the barrier between you and the reality, and because of this barrier, you remain confined in a dark cell where no light ever reaches and where no joy can ever penetrate. You live in misery because you are not meant to live in such a small, confined space. Your being wants to expand to the very ultimate source of existence. Your being longs to be oceanic, and you have become a dewdrop. How can you be happy? How can you be blissful? Man lives in misery because man lives imprisoned.

And Gautama the Buddha says that *tanha*—desire—is the root cause of all our misery because desire creates the mind. Desire means creating future, projecting yourself in the future, bringing tomorrow in. Bring the tomorrow in, and the today disappears, you cannot see it any longer, your eyes are clouded by the tomorrow. Bring the tomorrow in, and you will have to carry the load of all your yesterdays because the tomorrow can only be there if the yesterdays go on nourishing it.

Each desire is born out of the past, and each desire is projected in the future. The past and the future, they constitute your whole mind. Analyze the mind, dissect it, and you will find only two things: the past and the future. You will not find even an iota of the present, not even a single atom. And the present is the only reality, the only existence, the only dance there is.

The present can be found only when mind has ceased utterly—when the past no longer overpowers you and the future no more possesses you, when you are disconnected from the memories and the imaginations. In that moment where are you? Who are you? In that moment you are a nobody. And nobody can hurt you when you are a nobody. You cannot be wounded because the ego is very ready to receive wounds. The ego is almost seeking and searching to be wounded; it exists through wounds. Its whole existence depends on misery, pain.

When you are a nobody, anguish is impossible, anxiety is simply unbelievable. When you are a nobody, there is great silence, stillness, no noise inside. Past gone, future disappeared—what is there to create noise? And the silence that is heard is celestial, sacred. For the first time, in those spaces of no-mind, you become aware of the eternal celebration that goes on and on. That's what the existence is made of.

Except man, the whole existence is blissful. Only man has fallen out of it, has gone astray. Only man can do it because only man has consciousness.

Now, consciousness has two possibilities: It can become a bright light in you, so bright that even the sun will look pale compared to it—Buddha says if a thousand suns have risen suddenly, when you look within with no mind it is all light, eternal light. It is all joy, pure, uncontaminated, unpolluted. It is simple bliss, innocent. It is wonder. Its majesty is indescribable, its beauty inexpressible, and its benediction inexhaustible. *Aes dhammo sanantano*—"so is the ultimate law."

If you can only put your mind aside, you will become aware of the cosmic play. Then you are only energy, and the energy is always here now, it never leaves the "herenow." That is one possibility; you can become pure consciousness.

The other possibility is you can become self-consciousness. Then you fall. Then you become a separate entity from the world. Then you become an island, defined, well-defined. Then you are confined because all definitions confine. Then you are in a prison cell, and the prison cell is dark, utterly dark. There is no light, no possibility of light. And the prison cell cripples you, paralyzes you.

Self-consciousness becomes a bondage; the self is the bondage. And consciousness becomes freedom.

Drop the self and be conscious! That is the whole message, the message of all the buddhas of all the ages, past, present, future. The essential core of the message is very simple: Drop the self, the ego, the mind, and be.

Just this moment when this silence pervades, who are you? A nobody, a nonentity. You don't have a name, you don't have a form. You are neither man nor woman, neither Hindu nor Mohammedan. You don't belong to any country, to any nation, to any race. You are not the body, and you are not the mind.

Then what are you? In this silence, what is your taste? How does it taste to be? Just a peace, just a silence . . . and out of that peace and silence a great joy starts surfacing, welling up, for no reason at all. It is your spontaneous nature.

The art of putting the mind aside is the whole secret of religiousness because as you put the mind aside, your being explodes into a thousand and one colors. You become a rainbow, a lotus, a one-thousand-petaled lotus. Suddenly you open up, and then the whole beauty of existence—which is infinite—is yours. Then all the stars in the sky are within you. Then even the sky is not your limit; you no longer have any limits.

Silence gives you a chance to melt, merge, disappear, evaporate. And when you are not, you are; for the first time you are. When you are not, God is, nirvana is, enlightenment is. When you are not, all is found. When you are, all is lost.

Man has become a self-consciousness; that is his going astray, that is the original fall. All the religions talk about the original fall in some way or other, but the best story is contained in Christianity. The original fall is because man eats from the tree of knowledge. When you eat of the tree of knowledge, the fruits of knowledge, it creates self-consciousness.

The more knowledgeable you are, the more egoistic you are . . . hence the ego of the scholars, pundits, *maulvis*. The ego becomes decorated with great knowledge, scriptures, systems of thought. But they don't make you innocent; they don't bring you the childlike quality of openness, of trust, of love, of playfulness. Trust, love, playfulness, wonder all disappear when you become very knowledgeable.

And we are being taught to become knowledgeable. We are not taught to be innocent, we are not taught how to feel the wonder of existence. We are told the names of the flowers, but we are not taught how to dance around the flowers. We are told the names of the mountains, but we are not taught how to commune with the mountains, how to commune with the stars, how to commune with the trees, how to be in tune with existence.

Out of tune, how can you be happy? Out of tune, you are bound to remain in anguish, in great misery, in pain. You can be happy only when you are dancing with the dance of the whole, when you are just a part of the dance, when you are just a part of this great orchestra, when you are not singing your song separately. Only then, in that melting, is man free.

How can I stay myself? I feel I lose myself when I get really close to people.

Everybody wants to become extraordinary. That is the search of the ego: to be someone who is special, to be someone who is unique, incomparable. And this is the paradox: The more you try to be exceptional, the more ordinary you look because everybody is after extraordinariness. It is such an ordinary desire. If you become ordinary, the very search to be ordinary is extraordinary because rarely does somebody want to be just nobody, rarely does somebody want to be just a hollow, empty space.

This is really extraordinary in a way because nobody wants it. And when you become ordinary, you become extraordinary, and, of course, suddenly you discover that without searching you have become unique.

In fact, everybody is unique. If you can stop constantly running after goals for even a single moment, you will realize that you are unique. It is nothing to be discovered; it is already there. It is already the case: To be is to be unique. There is no other way of being. Every leaf on a tree is unique, every pebble on the shore is unique; there is no other way of being. You cannot find a similar pebble anywhere on the whole of the earth.

Two similar things do not exist at all, so there is no need to be somebody. You just be yourself, and suddenly you are unique, incomparable. That's why I say that this is a paradox: Those who search fail, and those who don't bother, suddenly attain.

But don't get confused in words. Let me repeat: The desire to be extraordinary is very ordinary because everybody has it. And to have the understanding to be ordinary is very extraordinary because it rarely happens. A Buddha, a Lao Tzu, a Jesus have it. To try to be unique is on everybody's mind and all these people fail and fail utterly.

How can you be more unique than you are already? Uniqueness is already there; you have to discover it. You are not to invent it; it is hidden within you. You have to expose it to existence, that's all. This uniqueness is not to be cultivated. It is your treasure. You have been carrying it for ever and ever. It is your very being, your very core of being. You just have to close your eyes and look at yourself. You have just to stop for a while and rest and look. But you are running so fast, you are in such great haste to achieve it, that you will miss it.

It is said by one of Lao Tzu's great disciples, Lieh Tzu, that once an idiot was searching for fire with a candle in his hand. Said Lieh

Tzu: "Had he known what fire was, he could have cooked his rice sooner. He remained hungry the whole night because he was searching for fire but couldn't find it, and he had a candle in his hand. How can you search in the dark without a candle?"

You are searching for uniqueness, and you have it in your hand. If you understand this, you can cook your rice sooner. I have cooked my rice and I know. You are unnecessarily hungry—the rice is there, the candle is there, the candle is fire. There is no need to take the candle and search. If you take a candle in your hand, and you go on searching all over the world, you will not find fire because you don't understand what fire is. Otherwise you would have understood because the candle was just in front of you, you were holding it in your hand.

It happens sometimes to people who use glasses. They have their glasses on, and they are searching for them. They may be in a hurry, and when they are in a hurry, they search everywhere and they completely forget that they have the glasses on. One can get in a panic. You may have had certain experiences like this in your life—because of the very search you become so panicky and so worried and so disturbed that your vision is no longer clear, and something that is just in front of you, you cannot see.

This is the case. You need not search for uniqueness; you are unique already. There is no way to make a thing more unique. The words "more unique" are absurd. Unique is enough, there exists nothing like "more unique." It is just like the word *circle*. Circles exist— there exists nothing like "more circular." That is absurd. A circle is always perfect; more is not needed. There are no degrees of circularity. A circle is a circle; less and more are useless.

Uniqueness is uniqueness; less and more don't apply to it. You are already unique. One realizes this only when one is ready to become ordinary. This is the paradox. But if you understand, there is no problem—the paradox is there, and beautiful, and no problem exists. A paradox is not a problem. It looks like a problem if you don't understand; if you understand, it is beautiful, a mystery.

Become ordinary, and you will become extraordinary. Try to become extraordinary and you will remain ordinary.

What is it to give and what is it to receive? I understand now that I am only just beginning to glimpse these. Receptiveness feels like dying to me, and automatically everything inside goes on red alert. Help! Existence seems so huge.

I can understand what is troubling you. It is troubling almost everybody. It is good that you have recognized it because now changing the situation is possible. Unfortunate are those who are suffering from the same problem but are not aware of it; because of their unawareness, there is no possibility of any transformation.

You have taken courage to expose yourself. I am immensely glad about it. I want all my people to be courageous enough to expose themselves, howsoever ugly it seems.

The conditioning is to go on hiding the ugly and go on pretending about the beautiful. That creates a schizophrenic situation: You go on showing yourself, what you are not; and you go on repressing yourself, what you are. Your life becomes a continuous civil war. You are fighting with yourself, and any fight with yourself is going to destroy you. Nobody can win.

If my right hand and left hand start fighting, do you think any hand can win? I can manage sometimes to let the right hand feel good as a winner, and sometimes to change the situation and let the left hand feel it is the winner. But neither can be really the winner because they both are my hands.

Almost every human being is carrying a split personality. And the most significant fact is that he identifies himself with the false part, and he denies his reality. In this situation you cannot hope to grow up as a spiritual being.

What the questioner is saying is tremendously important to understand. She is asking, "What is it to give?" Have you ever asked yourself what it is to give? You think you are already giving so much to your children, to your wife, to your girlfriend, to society, to the Rotary Club, to the Lions Club—you are giving so much. But the fact is, you don't know what it is to give.

Unless you give yourself, you don't give at all.

You can give money, but you are not the money. Unless you give yourself—that means unless you give love—you don't know what giving is.

". . . and what is it to receive?" Almost everybody thinks he knows what it is to receive. But the questioner is right in questioning and exposing herself, that she does not know what it is to receive. Just as unless you give love you don't know what it is to give, the same is true about receiving: Unless you are capable of receiving love, you don't know what it is to receive. You want to be loved, but you have not thought about it: Are you capable of receiving love? There are so many hindrances that won't allow you to receive it.

The first is, you don't have any self-respect; hence when love comes toward you, you don't feel yourself adequate enough to receive it. But you are in such a mess that you cannot even see a simple fact: Because you have never accepted yourself as you are, you have never loved yourself, how can you manage to receive somebody else's love?

You know you are not worthy of it, but you don't want to accept and recognize this stupid idea that has been fed to you, that you are not worthy of it. So what do you do? You simply refuse love. And to refuse love, you have to find excuses.

The first and the most prominent excuse is, "It is not love—that's why I cannot accept it." You cannot believe that somebody can love you. When you yourself cannot love you, when you have not seen yourself, your beauty and your grace and your grandeur, how can you believe it when somebody says, "You are beautiful. I can see in your eyes a depth, unfathomable, of tremendous grace. I can see in your heart a rhythm, in tune with the universe." You cannot believe all this; it is too much. You are accustomed to being condemned, you are accustomed to being punished, you are accustomed to being rejected. You are accustomed to not being accepted as you are—so these things you can take very easily.

Love will have a tremendous impact on you because you will have to go through a great transformation before you can receive it. First you have to accept yourself without any guilt. You are not a sinner as the Christians and other religions go on teaching you.

You don't see the stupidity of the whole thing. Some guy far away in the past, one Adam, disobeyed God, which is not much of a sin. In fact, he was absolutely right to disobey him. If anybody had committed a sin, it was God, by prohibiting his own son, his own daughter, from eating the fruit of knowledge and eating the fruit of eternal life. What kind of father? What kind of God? What kind of love?

Love demands that God should have told Adam and Eve, "Before you eat anything else, these two trees have to be remembered. Eat as much from the tree of wisdom and eat as much from the tree of eternal life as you like, so that you can also be in the same space of immortality in which I am." That should be a simple thing for anyone who loves.

But God prohibiting Adam from wisdom means he wants him to remain ignorant. Perhaps he is jealous, afraid, apprehensive that if Adam becomes wise, he will become equal to him. He wants to keep Adam in his ignorance so that he remains inferior. And if he eats the fruit of eternal life, then he will be a god himself.

This God who prevented Adam and Eve must have been very jealous, utterly ugly, inhuman, unloving. And if all these things are not sin, then what can sin be? But religions have been teaching you, Jews and Christians and Mohammedans, that you are still carrying the sin that Adam committed. There is a limit to stretching lies out so long. Even if Adam had committed a sin, you cannot carry it. You were created by God, according to these religions, and you are not carrying godliness, but you are carrying Adam and Eve's disobedience?

This is the Western way to condemn you—you are a sinner. The Eastern way comes to the same conclusion but from different premises. They say everybody is loaded with immense sin and evil deeds, committed in millions of past lives. In fact, the burden of a Christian or a Jew or a Mohammedan is far less. You are only carrying the sin that Adam and Eve committed. And it must have become very diluted—centuries upon centuries. You are not a direct inheritor of Adam and Eve's sins. It has passed through many millions of hands; by now the quantity must be almost homeopathic.

But the Eastern concept is even more dangerous. You are not carrying somebody else's sin. In the first place you cannot carry somebody else's sin. Your father commits a crime—you cannot be sent to jail. Even ordinary human common sense will say that if the father has committed the sin or the crime, he has to suffer. The son or the grandson cannot be sent to the gallows because the grandfather committed a murder.

But the Eastern concept is much more dangerous and poisonous:

It is your own sin that you are carrying, not that of Adam and Eve. And it is not a small quantity; it has been growing with each life! And you have lived millions of lives before this life, and in each life you have committed so many sins. They are all accumulated on your chest. The burden is Himalayan; you are crushed under it.

This is a strange strategy to destroy your dignity, to reduce you into a subhuman being. How can you love yourself? You can hate, but you cannot love. How can you think that somebody may be able to love you? It is better to reject it because sooner or later the person who is offering you his love is going to discover your reality, which is very ugly—just a long, long burden of sin. And then that person is going to reject you. To avoid rejection, it is better to reject love. That's why people don't accept love.

They desire, they long for it. But when the moment comes and somebody is ready to shower you with love, you shrink back. Your shrinking has a deep psychology. You are afraid: This is beautiful, but how long will it last? Sooner or later my reality will be revealed. It is better from the very beginning to be alert.

Love means intimacy, love means two persons coming closer, love means two bodies but one soul. You are afraid: Your soul? A sinner's soul, burdened with the evil deeds of millions of lives? No, it is better to hide it; it is better not to come into a position where the person who wanted to love you rejects you. It is the fear of rejection that does not allow you to receive love.

You cannot give love because nobody has ever told you that you are born a loving being. They have told you, "You are born in sin!" You cannot love, and you cannot receive love, either. This has diminished all possibilities of your growth.

The questioner is saying, "I understand now that I am only just beginning to glimpse these." You are fortunate because there are millions of people in the world who have become completely blind to their own conditionings, the ugly burdens that the older generation has given them. It is hurting so much that it is better to forget all about it. But by forgetting it, you cannot remove it.

By forgetting a cancer, you cannot operate upon it. By not recognizing it, keeping it in the dark, you are taking the greatest unnecessary risk against yourself. It will go on growing. It needs darkness; it needs you to not know about it. It will cover up your whole being sooner or later. And nobody else will be responsible for it except you.

So if you feel that you are having glimpses, a few windows are opening in you.

"Receptiveness feels like dying to me . . ." Have you ever thought about it? Receptiveness feels like dying to you—it is true. Receptiveness feels like dying because receptiveness looks like humiliation. To receive something, particularly love, means you are a beggar. Nobody wants to be on the receiving end because that makes you inferior to the giver. "Receptiveness feels like dying to me, and automatically everything inside goes on red alert."

This red alert is implanted in you by the society that you have always respected, by the same people you have thought were your well-wishers. And I don't say that they are intentionally trying to harm you. They have been harmed by others, and they are simply transferring whatsoever they have received from their parents, from their teachers, from the older generation.

Each generation goes on giving its diseases to the new generation, and naturally the new generation becomes more and more burdened. You are the inheritor of all the superstitious, repressive concepts of the whole of history. What goes on red alert is not something that belongs to you. It is your conditioning that goes on red alert. And your last sentence is just an effort to find a rationalization for it. That is also one of the great dangers everybody has to be aware of.

Don't rationalize.

Go to the very root of every problem.

But don't find excuses because if you find excuses, you cannot remove those roots.

The last statement of the questioner is a rationalization. Perhaps she has not been able to see its intrinsic quality. She says, "Help! Existence seems so huge."

Now she is thinking that she is afraid of receiving because existence is so huge, that she is afraid of giving because existence is so huge. What is the point of giving your small love, just like a dewdrop, to the ocean? The ocean will never know about it; hence there is no point in giving and there is no point in receiving, either. Because the ocean is so huge, you will be drowned in it. Hence it looks like death. But this is your rationalization.

You don't know anything about existence; you don't know anything about yourself—which is the closest point of existence to you. Unless you start from your own being, you will never know existence. That is the starting point, and everything has to begin from the very beginning.

Knowing yourself, you will know your existence. But the taste and the fragrance of your existence will give you courage to go a little deeper into the existence of others. If your own existence has made you so blissful, it is a natural longing to enter into other mysteries that surround you: human mysteries, mysteries of the animals, mysteries of the trees, mysteries of the stars.

And once you have known your existence, you are no longer afraid of death.

Death is a fiction; it does not happen, it only appears. It appears from the outside. Have you ever seen your own death? You have always seen somebody else dying. But have you seen yourself dying? Nobody has; otherwise even this minimum of life would become impossible. You see, every day somebody dies, but it is always somebody else; it is never you.

The poet who wrote "Never ask for whom the bell tolls; it tolls for thee" has a deeper understanding than you. He must have been a Christian because when somebody dies in a Christian village, the church bell rings to inform everybody—people who have gone to their farms, to their orchards, people who have gone to work somewhere. The church bell reminds them: Somebody has died. So they all have to come back to give the last farewell.

But the poet has a tremendous insight when he says, "Never ask for whom the bell tolls. It tolls for thee."

In your actual life it never rings for thee. One day it will ring, but then you will no longer be here to hear it. You never think of yourself at the threshold of death—and everybody is standing on the threshold. You always see somebody else dying, hence the experience is objective, not subjective.

The other is not really dying, only changing houses. His life force is moving into a new form, into a new plane. Only the body is left without life energy—but the body never had it.

It is just like in a dark house when a candle is burning and the whole house is lit. Even from the outside you can see the light from the windows, from the doors, but the house does not have the light as an intrinsic part of it. The moment the candle finishes, the house will be in darkness. In fact, it has always been in darkness; it was the candle that was the light.

Your body is already dead. What gives you the impression that it is alive is your life force, your being, which radiates through the body, which fills the body with aliveness. All that you have seen when people die is that something has disappeared. You don't know where it has gone—whether it has actually gone anywhere or simply ceased to be. So from the outside the fiction of death has been created.

Those who have known themselves know without any doubt that they are eternal beings. They have died many times, yet they are alive.

Death and birth are only small episodes in the great pilgrimage of the soul. Your fear of death will disappear immediately the moment you come in contact with yourself. And that opens up a totally new sky to be explored. Once you know that there is no death, all fear disappears. The fear of the unknown, the fear of the dark . . . whatever the form, all fears disappear. You start for the first time being a real adventurer. You start moving into different mysteries that surround you.

Existence becomes for the first time your home.

There is nothing to be feared: It is your mother; you are part of it. It cannot drown you, it cannot destroy you.

The more you know it, the more you will feel nourished; the more you know it, the more you will feel blessed; the more you know it, the more you will be. Then you can give love because you have it. And then you can receive love because there is no question of rejection.

Your question will be helpful to everybody. I thank you for your question and for your courage to expose yourself. This courage is needed by everyone because without this courage, you cannot hope for any possibility of transformation—into a new world, into a new consciousness, into your authentic being, which is the door to ultimate reality and to ultimate benediction.

INTIMACY

What is the real answer to living in intimacy?

To know existence, you have to be existential. You are not existential, you live in thoughts. You live in the past, in the future, but never here and now. And existence is right here now. You are not here, hence the question arises. The question arises because of you not meeting with existence. You think you live, but you don't live. You think you love, but you don't love. You only think about love, you think about life, you think about existence, and that very thinking is the question, that thinking is a barrier. Drop all thoughts and see. You will not find a single question; only the answer exists.

That's why I insist again and again that the search is not really for the answer, the search is not really so that your questions can be answered. No, the search is only about how to drop the questions, how to see life and existence with a nonquestioning mind. That is the meaning of *shraddha,* trust. This is the deepest dimension of *shraddha* or trust—you look at existence with a nonquestioning mind.

You simply look. You have no idea how to look at it, you don't impose any form on it, you don't have any prejudice; you simply look with naked eyes, absolutely uncovered by any thoughts, any philosophies, any religions. You look at existence with eyes like a small child, and then suddenly there is only the answer.

There are no questions in existence. Questions come from you. And they will go on coming, and you can go on accumulating as many answers as you like; those answers won't help. You have to attain to the answer—and to attain to the answer, you have to drop all questioning. When there is no question in the mind, the vision is clear, you have a clarity of perception; the doors of perception are clean and open, and everything suddenly becomes transparent. You can go to the very depth. Wherever you look, your look penetrates to the deepest core—and there suddenly you find yourself.

You find yourself everywhere. You will find yourself in a rock if you look deep, deep enough. Then the looker, the observer, becomes the observed, the seer becomes the seen, the knower becomes the known. If you look deep enough in a rock, in a tree, or in a man or in a woman, if you go on looking deeply, that look is a circle. It starts from you, then passes through the other and comes back to you. Everything is so transparent. Nothing hinders. The ray goes, becomes a circle, and falls back on you.

Hence one of the greatest secret sentences of the Upanishads: *Tat Tïwamasi Swetaketu*: "Thou art that" or "That art thou." The circle is complete. Now the devotee is one with God. Now the seeker is one with the sought. Now the inquirer himself becomes the answer.

In existence there is no question. I have lived in it long enough now, and I haven't come across a single question—not even a fragment of a question. One simply lives it.

Then life has a beauty of its own. No doubt arises in the mind, no suspicion surrounds you, no question exists within your being—you are undivided, whole.

About the Author

✿

Osho is a contemporary mystic whose life and teachings have influenced millions of people of all ages and from all walks of life. He has been described by the *Sunday Times* in London as one of the "1,000 Makers of the 20th Century" and by the *Sunday Mid-Day* (India) as one of the ten people—along with Gandhi, Nehru, and Buddha—who have changed the destiny of India.

About his own work Osho has said that he is helping to create the conditions for the birth of a new kind of human being. He has often characterized this new human being as "Zorba the Buddha"—capable of enjoying both the earthy pleasures of a Zorba the Greek and the silent serenity of a Gautama the Buddha. Running like a thread through all aspects of Osho's work is a vision that encompasses both the timeless wisdom of the East and the highest potential of Western science and technology.

He is also known for his revolutionary contribution to the science of inner transformation, with an approach to meditation that acknowledges the accelerated pace of contemporary life. His unique "Active Meditations" are designed to first release the accumulated stresses of body and mind, so that it is easier to experience the thought-free and relaxed state of meditation.

Meditation Resort

❧

Osho Commune International

O sho Commune International, the meditation resort that Osho established in India as an oasis where his teachings could be put into practice, continues to attract thousands of visitors per year from more than one hundred different countries around the world. Located about one hundred miles southeast of Bombay in Pune, India, the facilities cover thirty-two acres in a tree-lined suburb known as Koregaon Park. The resort provides limited accommodation for guests, but there is a plentiful variety of nearby hotels.

The resort meditation programs are based on Osho's vision of a qualitatively new kind of human being who is able both to participate joyously in everyday life and to relax into silence. Most programs take place in modern, air-conditioned facilities and include everything from short to extended meditation courses, creative arts, holistic health treatments, personal growth, and the "Zen" approach to sports and recreation. Programs are offered throughout the year, alongside a full daily schedule of Osho's active meditations.

Outdoor cafes and restaurants within the resort grounds serve both traditional Indian fare and a variety of international dishes, all made with organically grown vegetables from the commune's own farm. The campus has its own private supply of safe, filtered water.

For more information: www.osho.com

This is a comprehensive Web site in different languages, featuring an online tour of the meditation resort, travel information, information about books and tapes, Osho information centers worldwide, and selections from Osho's talks.

Osho International
New York
e-mail: oshointernational@oshointernational.com
web: www.osho.com/oshointernational